"Reading *Poetry Power* by Melanie Faith—chock-full of humour, personal asides, and sensible, doable suggestions to improve one's writing—I felt a continual urge to write and revise my poems. A perfect guide for the poet who wants a refresher course in the basics of this 'little genre' (and a few photography hints) from a new point of view and who needs a nudge to live more deliberately, Faith's book reminds me of an intimate conversation between two engaged introverts for whom layers of complicated interior depth—juxtaposed in the 'nooks and crannies' of dreams and fragments of memory—hold the key to discovery and development of a unique, artistic voice that rings with universality." HELEN LOSSE, AUTHOR OF *EVERY TENDER REED*

"This is the definitive book on, for, and about poetry. Melanie more than delivers on the promise she made in the Introduction: *This book is meant to reach you where you are and to withstand multiple readings as you explore your individual writer's path.* Indeed! I find that no matter what funk I'm in, I open *Poetry Power* and I discover my next step on my poetry journey. I know my fellow poets will too!" MARI L. MCCARTHY, INTERNATIONAL BEST-SELLING AUTHOR OF *JOURNALING POWER: HOW TO CREATE THE HAPPY, HEALTHY LIFE YOU WANT TO LIVE!*

"'I am not a poet.' Having believed this for years, I was hesitant when Melanie asked me to read her book, *Poetry Power*. Since I love to read poetry, I said 'Of course.' After reading *Poetry Power*, I feel confident that yes! I could be a poet. Melanie takes her readers by the hand and walks them through the whole process of writing, publishing, editing and loving poetry. Little personal vignettes scattered throughout *Poetry Power* made me feel like Melanie was a friend. It was as if we were in a writing group together and she was sharing her writing secrets. Each chapter ends with a *Try this Prompt* that are easy and exciting to try. They range from something that might take a few minutes, to others that were more involved. In my second, third, and so on readings of *Poetry Power* I will jump into the prompts with feet, hands and heart. I am already making a list of the people I will be purchasing a copy of *Poetry Power* for—and they include writers from all genres, not just poets. This is a book that all writers will benefit from reading." TRICIA L. MCDONALD, WRITER AND CEO *SPLATTERED INK PRESS*

About the Author

Melanie Faith is an English professor, tutor, and freelance writing consultant whose writing has been nominated for three Pushcart Prizes. She loves writing and teaching in several genres, including flash fiction and nonfiction, poetry, creative nonfiction, novel-writing, and craft articles about the writing process. She holds an MFA from Queens University of Charlotte. Her photographs have been featured on literary magazine covers and on books of poetry. In her free time, she collects quotes, books, and shoes; learns about still-life photography and the Tiny-House movement; and travels to spend time with her darling nieces.

To learn more about Melanie, visit: *melaniedfaith.com*

POETRY POWER

An Interactive Guide for Writing, Editing, Teaching, and Reflecting on the Life Poetic

MELANIE FAITH

Vine Leaves Press
Melbourne, Vic, Australia

Print Edition
ISBN: 978-1-925417-80-7

Published by Vine Leaves Press 2018
Melbourne, Victoria, Australia

Cover design by Jessica Bell
Interior design by Amie McCracken

 A catalogue record for this book is available from the National Library of Australia

Table of Contents

Introductory Note from Your Author:
Why Write Poetry?

- I don't understand it. It makes no sense.

- My teacher ruined poetry for me in high school.

- It's just so boring.

- It has too many rules.

- It's so random. When should I break a line or a stanza?

- I attended a workshop where everybody was a jerk. They tore apart my work. Never again.

- I'm better at fiction.

- It's confusing. Just come out and say what you mean in plain English.

- It's by a bunch of dead white guys and doesn't connect to my life.

- There aren't characters or a story in it.

- I tried, but I lose interest.

- Why spend so much time learning it? Nobody pays for poetry, like novels.

Sound familiar? I've been a practicing poet since I was 18 and a teacher for over 20 years. I've heard combinations of all of this reasoning (and sometimes, multiple combinations of these answers from the same student or friend in one sitting) when people learn that I write and teach poetry and then launch into why they love to write and read this or that genre but *don't* write or read poetry (usually with either an apologetic or slightly scowling face).

While I assure you I'm not the poetry police and won't be calling you to the board and making you recite a sonnet anytime soon, I do feel passion and enthusiasm for my little genre that could. **Poetry is an art form that takes a lifetime to learn and yet, you don't need to know a lot to get started. In fact, you already know a lot more about poetry than you think.** Anyone ever sung you a nursery rhyme? Sung along with lyrics? Recited those rhymey jingles for products? There's a bit of poetry in all of these and in much of the language that surrounds you in your everyday life.

Poetry is compact, and it's multi-layered. Poetry teaches us to pay attention, to look our environments and other people in the eye and truly see what is there—or what isn't. **Like all art forms that are condensed and jam-packed with meaning, it gives back to its creator as much as it offers to its readers**.

Poetry is beautifully revelatory. It will show you

thoughts about yourself and your world that you never even knew were running through your subconscious.

Poetry is a symbiotic relationship. Your poetry will grow—in theme, topic, style, and imagery—as you stretch and progress in life. Unlike some friendships or relationships, you won't outgrow it; you'll coincide and inform it, and it you. What amazing dividends, and what a gift to offer a world sorely in need of reflection at a slower and more thoughtful pace!

As Vincent Van Gogh once noted: "Poetry surrounds us everywhere, but putting it on paper is, alas, not so easy as looking at it." I designed this book with both the struggles and the joys of the practicing poet in mind. Think of this as your own inspiration station, and you're about to set off—not from one stop to another, but on numerous, ongoing, and revelatory journeys in one. Whether you choose to read this book chronologically or topically, there's plenty of companionship to be found as well as motivation for the days when you don't even feel like setting pen to paper, but you will … you will.

This all sounds well and good coming from a fancy MFA program grad, but what about real-world advice? What about tips we can actually take with us and use as we look for ideas, write our first drafts, attempt editing, or send out our first shaky drafts? What about that? Yes, what about that? This book will assist you in all of these areas of the poetic journey … and more, with some fantastic poetry intermingled with recommendations for poems from the past two hundred years and versifiers from diverse backgrounds and perspectives.

Care for some writing prompts specifically tailored to the poetic writing journey? Each chapter ends with them. Prefer analysis of what a real-life, successful, thematic poem has done that we might apply to our own poems? You'll find a helping of that here. Feel like some quotation inspiration? Yep, there's a smattering of that in these pages, too.

So, why poetry? No. Why *not* poetry?

Whether you've been penning poems for 50 years or if you've just decided to venture into the warm waters of verse for the first time this year, **this book is meant to reach you where you are and to withstand multiple readings as you explore your individual writer's path.**

Long may you savour this journey. Happy poetizing!

Section I
Making Your Way in the World Today: Tools and Techniques

Lockets: Set to Work with the Mighty Small

Lockets. Not merely pendants that open on tiny hinges, they are well-crafted relics from another, slower time. Formed of precious metals in the shapes of ovals, squares, circles, or (often) hearts, they might be engraved with designs or initials on the outside. Unlike most jewels, however, the outside appearance is secondary.

As perhaps our mothers reassured us: *it's what's inside that counts*. Inside, a small compartment might contain a tiny photograph of a baby or a sweetheart or a folded message in script on a scrap of paper or a lock of hair from a love, a pebble, colourful threads given (or taken), or another tiny treasure. Highly personal meaning is the point of a locket, after all. Worn in public, but mostly private.

While lockets were used for centuries as amulets, they became a wildly popular fashion statement in the Victorian era—a suppressive era when communications were oblique and often expressed in flower bouquets that ascribed symbolic meaning by blossom name (striped carnations for indecision or a *maybe* reply, yellow carnations for no, pink roses for friendship and admiration, purple roses for enchantment, sweet peas for departure, zinnias for thoughts of absent friends, palms for victory, moss for maternal love, violets for faithful love), formal calling cards were expected before a visit, and necklines and hemlines left almost the entire body to the imagination. In such a culture, people had to work hard to prove trustworthiness to earn even a glimpse into another person's personal life.

There's a surprisingly healthy market for these jewels online.

In fact, various artisans make and sell brand-new lockets via their websites. K.L., who started out painting large canvasses, surprised herself one day, buying some plain circular lockets in which she practiced painting through several layers over a year. Many of her lockets are filled with celestial designs of comets, moons, and constellations. In a video about her work as a craftsperson, she notes how appealing lockets are—a secret, personal world available at any time—a bit like Narnia's wardrobe.

A space in which we don't post? [Gasp.] Now *that's* refreshing in an era of endless ways to broadcast, announce, reveal, and reprimand. We often think what we see posted online is the fullness of a person's life story, but rarely is that the case. Many struggles are never posted. Likely that's why these jewels are experiencing a resurgence—they remind us of a multitude of contradictory layers to being human and, as much as we like to share, certain places and experiences that best remain entirely personal or expressed only in evocative, edited snippets.

Like lockets, poetry is a purposefully petite artform. Compression and focus are key parts of the

art. Just as you can't cram a bureau shelf of treasures inside a single, narrow locket, you don't chuck every disparate, random idea and feeling into a single poem. Poems are neither inconsequential nor cute—they are highly sophisticated communiqués.

Few poets understood that as well as **Issa and Basho**, two masters of haiku, senryū (similar to haiku, with 17 syllables, but often comical or about human nature), and Tanka (a 31-syllable, five-line unrhymed poem). Here are two of my favourite classic poems from each poet that illustrate the might of the mini.

> "Don't worry spiders
> I keep house
> casually."
> —Issa
>
> "Why so scrawny, cat?
> starving for fat fish
> or mice . . .
> Or backyard love?"
> —Basho

Issa's poem relies on a single, final punch-line word, "casually," to deliver humour. Many comics and humour writers have noted the importance of concluding a statement, line, or sentence with a humorous twist word or phrase that is unexpected. Had Issa written "casually" in the second line, before "keep" and ended on "house" the effect wouldn't have been nearly as funny. Word order (syntax) is vital to verse.

Basho's piece begins with a colloquially phrased, down-to-earth question of an animal—a quirky, catchy set up that could lead us to wry places. He then offers three quick possibilities for this stray feline—food, food, and (what's this?) love. **Delivering a third, unexpected item in a series does the trick.** Again, humour, and yet … maybe not. The modifier "backyard" can be a place image or it might be a stab at ribald funniness. Perhaps he's suggesting by noticing that he, too, has longed for a love, no matter how short-lived. Either way, it works quite well.

Both of these poems offer the fleeting thoughts and feelings of two writers centuries ago; vulnerability and humanity shine in their finely crafted musings that resonate through time.

On par with origami and chef-made truffles or pastry, each piece is carefully composed and presented but provides no less insight or appreciation for having been crafted. Poetry offers the opportunity to offer a focused glimpse at your internal landscape—as much or as little as you care to share.

Poetry reminds us that it is a wise idea to leave some of life un-broadcast. Refraining from excessive posting may enhance personal development, happiness, and even peace of mind. Paradoxically, by taking time to pull back and search inwardly to organize and sculpt our thoughts, fears, and hopes into poems, we will create art that can connect in a deeper way when we feel ready to share again.

These two poets don't share everything with their audiences—but ah, what they do! Don't you get a feeling for each poet's personality from their versifying? From specific circumstances and images to timeless jewels we find resonant with our own experiences. Not bad. Not bad at all.

Try this Prompt! Write a short poem in any form where the last line, phrase, or word creates a subtle shift in the poem's tone or adds humour, as in Issa's and Basho's work. No worries if you don't initially deliver the ha-ha in your first draft (comedic writers frequently sweat through numerous drafts to get the final laughs); take as many drafts as you need to sculpt that final zinger. Go!

Embracing Beginner's Mind: Six Tips for Poetic Openings

"IN THE BEGINNER'S MIND THERE ARE MANY POSSIBILITIES BUT IN THE EXPERT'S THERE ARE FEW." —SHUNRYU SUZUKI

One of my students recently wrote a riveting essay about his first few days at a boarding school in America. At 16, he was awash in firsts. First airplane rides, during which he jostled between connecting flights and airports by himself, halfway around the world from his home; first time having a roommate not related to him and from another culture and religion; first time communicating and studying daily in a language not his own, a third language he'd practiced for merely a year or two before coming to the US.

I marvelled, after reading his experiences, at how nerve-wracking that culture shock must have been for him, not having the vocabulary nor the chance to ask for help privately.

In the West, we tend to think of beginnings as a real grind, testing our patience and skills, causing stress or embarrassment, and they *can* often be that way. On the other hand, beginnings present opportunities, as in the Eastern term *beginner's mind*. Much like children's minds as they explore the world without preconceived notions, adults can also embrace life open-heartedly and with enthusiasm.

Each poem we write is a new experience, one which carries the seeds of teaching us more about ourselves, others, and our surroundings. Each poem also provides the chance to communicate new or favourite ideas, hopes, and dreams. Writing is a lifelong apprenticeship with marvel, piece by piece, opening by opening.

Take one of these ideas for a spin as you consider your next poetic opening.

- **Begin with a line of dialogue**, heard or imagined, that acquaints the reader with the speaker's or narrator's POV. Yes, poems may use dialogue, too, just like their prose cousins.

- **Open with a thematic quote, called an epigraph**, as I did with this chapter. Epigraphs connect the reader to the theme and foreground it. Your poem may explicate the epigraph's idea more deeply, disagree with it completely, or move in a subtly different direction.

- **Start with a line of scenery to orient the reader into your poetic world and/or setting.** Maybe your poem begins at the kitchen table where a mother and son are putting vinegar into a dough volcano. Or maybe your speaker is atop a burrow descending a trail into an arroyo.

- **Attract with a resonant image.** If I were to write

a poem based on my student's first American experiences, I might open with the glint of a school crest engraved on the knife's handle as it's held aloft a bone-china plate.

- **Set up a comparison and contrast.** For the same poem idea about my student's experiences, I could open with a meal my student shared in comfort at home with his siblings in the first stanza and then segue into his first days struggling to make small talk in the dining hall for the second or third stanza.

- **Go to a poetry database online, such as www. poets.org, and read eight or 10 poems to study how other authors open their poems. Pay particular attention to first and second lines. What kind of diction choices do they make to hook the reader? Borrow one of the first lines to get you started.** Don't worry—your poem is sure to veer off to a unique destination.

Like my student, when you are unsure of how to begin, observe your options and then delve in, adjusting as you go based on the material and the poem's needs as you discover them.

Keep in mind, too, that **a beginning isn't necessarily forever—it's a way into the poem, to launch you; it may or may not be the final draft's start.**

Try this Prompt! Write a poem where you or your speaker was a fish-out-of-water in a new experience. What happened? How did you learn to adjust and/or fit in? Provide an image, dialogue, or scenery details.

Will the Real Speaker Please Stand up?

When I was a teenager, there was a game show that aired in the early evening called *To Tell the Truth*. In each episode, a series of celebrity panellists, often comics and actors, would listen to three seemingly ordinary contestants, all claiming to be the same person.

Each of three contestants, two fibbers and one truth-teller, would begin with the same claim, such as: "My name is Kelly Burns, and my shop sells the world's largest cupcakes." The celebrity panellists would then ask questions—sometimes serious and sometimes outlandish—to gauge who the real person belonging to the attribute might be before making a guess in front of a studio audience. The celebrity might quip, "What got you into the cupcake game, sweetie?" or "What's your best-selling flavour?" or "Just how big *are* your cupcakes?" or any number of oddball and entertaining queries that may or may not make the contestants fumble.

Sometimes, based on body language, facial expression, or tone of voice, the liar was easy to pinpoint. Other times, not so much, especially since even people telling the truth tend to trip over their words if they're not used to being on camera or if the question catches them off guard.

Part of the fun of watching the show was listening to the strange questions. Guessing right along also proved enjoyable, seeing if I could judge context clues, such as voice inflection, better than the celebrity panellists. I was often surprised at the results when the announcer asked the real so-and-so to please stand up.

Only as an adult did I learn that the show originated in the mid-1950s and lasted until the late 1960s in its first run. Several reboots have popped up since, including the season I watched. Clearly, people have a natural streak of curiosity when it comes to matters of potential faking and fibbing. We all like to think we can quickly gather the clues and not be fooled, but most of us—at least a portion of the time—make errors in judgment and guess incorrectly when reading context.

When I was a grad student, we workshopped our poems once a month. One of the first rules when verbally discussing other poets' work was that we not assume first-person poems were describing the author. In fact, **persona poems in first-person could just as likely be from a character's POV or another real-life person's POV speaking about his or her life experience.** Katie Bickham's first book, *The Belle Mar* (Pleiades 2015), is an excellent example of persona poetry. Her collection, set in a Louisiana plantation house, tells the story from the multiple perspectives of the slaves, women, children, and masters who pass through the home.

In order to address the poem's first-person nature (especially when workshopping), we spoke of "the speaker," instead of "you." This, at first, seemed a bit of sleight of hand and kind of clunky to remember to say. In the long term and as a teacher, this phrase proves ingenious and handy, especially when approaching others' drafts.

What are the advantages to penning poems with a speaker not ourselves? First person is an immediate POV. It deposits the writer and reader inside the skin of the protagonist telling the poem. **First person tends to be dynamic and focused. Third person is a bit removed;** more like a well-informed announcer. **It's the difference between writing a character and writing *about* a character.** While third-person POV can be all-knowing, first-person POV includes a limited scope that readers find compelling often because of their myopia, partialities, and limited understanding and viewpoint. While consternating in real people, flaws are intriguing and often gripping on the page.

Even if a poem is based on real-life events, poets should not be constrained to present a poem from their own viewpoints. "But that's the way it happened!" we're tempted to argue. True, but that one fact or event might just be the starting point while the entire rest of the poem is made-up; as readers, it is not our business to know. **There may be emotional truths equal to or superseding external truths** and, as we all know from having played telephone as children, even facts can shape-shift when told from person to person.

As writers, we would be wise, both in our own work and in approaching others' drafts, to acknowledge that each poem has a narrator—a speaker—who presents the poem from a unique position which may be part, whole, or not at all the poet.

Try this Prompt! Choose three poems—new or old, written by someone you know or a poet you only know through their published work—and make a note about the speaker. Does the author use first person? Second person "you" (which can have a jarring, bossy tone that grabs readers' attention)? Third person? What is the effect of the speaker's POV on readers? Which do you prefer, and why? How would the poem's tone, context, or content be different if written in another POV? Then choose a draft of one of your poems and change the speaker of the poem. What does this new speaker believe, see, or feel that alters your poem?

Origins, or: Black Friday Fever and a Spit Vial

Here's a first: two weeks ago, I found myself spitting into a vial which I then added a pale-bluish solution to and did a 30-second shake-shake-shake. Then, I slipped the "sample" (a term which always makes me cringe and think of faeces which this, happily, wasn't) into a sealed pouch that went into a sturdy, palm-sized box and off it sailed to the West Coast lab.

Why did you take this DNA test? you might well ask. It could have been Black Friday fever. While many shoppers lined up late Thanksgiving night for steals on sweaters, shoes, and electronics, I purchased a saliva kit and a mystery report. No, I didn't set even a pinkie toe into a box store, but I partook in the relaxing bargains-at-a-click that is also 2017 shopping. While checking social media, I noticed a sale ad for a company that markets a test to tell genetic-makeup in percentages and nationalities. Actually, "noticed" would be putting it too mildly: every third click-bait ad was from this particular company. Not exactly subtle. Then again, the price (as they say) was right and I had some PayPal funds from a freelance-editing gig available, so the test was almost free to me. Win-win, and it was on.

But it's more than just successful, repetitive advertising. It's a penchant to *know*. Sure, I've gone to plenty of family reunions. My Great Aunt Beulah traced my mother's paternal family back to the mid-1800s Germany, so about a quarter of me prefers schnitzel with noodles. My mother's maternal line, according to my Great Grandma Virginia, was proudly Scots-Irish. Potatoes and possibly a penchant for warrior-men in kilts and *Macbeth*, I can dig it. Still, that leaves out a lot of potential background information and endless possibilities. Yes, I might be mostly two or three (or four?) nationalities, but perhaps I'm a smidgeon Norwegian, despite my dark hair and eyes. Or a dash Spanish? Or decidedly British (that would explain my fixation with Dame Judy Dench, BBC adaptations of novels and *Victoria*, and my daily tea, although not the sugar instead of milk, would it, mate)?

"How do you know it's accurate?" a friend asks, when I confide my big purchase. "They could tell you anything."

True. It's sent from a lab, so to my non-scientific self that sounds legit, but still—I suppose it's possible there's some chicanery, since they're selling the test results, after all. Then again, why would the lab lie? I'm neither a celebrity nor the kind of person who will seek to refute whatever the test shows.

Either way, I'm not concerned. What I know for sure is that I'll have a new idea—a snippet of backstory, another way of viewing how I got from then to here and maybe where I'm headed—all for about 50 bucks with the sale and my credit. Not too shabby.

Another reason I might have hopped onto the DNA-test train is that it was just two weeks from the New Year. Ah, yes, that potent time to set goals for what is possible in the 12 fresh calendar pages ahead but also a time to think about how much time has passed. This week, I snagged an additional deal of the holiday season—a plane ticket to visit my darling nieces in July. By then, I'll know much more, according to the company's site, about those fabulous (faceless) forerunners.

In six to eight weeks, depending on demand (they are careful to note variable wait times in their online registration), I'll receive the full deets on just how much of me might be South American (no wonder I enjoy Bossa Nova music!), Moroccan (pass me a Fez!), French-Canadian (I studied the language for five years, after all) or some other nationality I haven't yet thought to connect to yours truly.

Look, origins have a powerful hold over our imaginations and our place in the world. They contain suggestions of time forgotten as well as time yet to be and what it means to be connected to various groups of people—or what we want it to mean.

Poets have long sung praises longing for connection as well as deeply moving indictments to forefathers and/or interlopers. Poets often address familial or tribal identity, heartbreak (individual or collective), customs, and/or invaders. Excellent examples include: Margaret Walker's "For My People," Ofelia Zepeda's "Carrying Our Words," Sherman Alexie's "How to Write the Great American Indian Novel," Juan Felipe Herrera's "Five Directions to My House," and Oscar

Gonzales' "We All Return to the Place Where We Were Born." Poetry collections to study include Joy Harjo's *In Mad Love and War* and *A Map to the Next World: Poetry & Tales* as well as Simon J. Ortiz's *Speaking for the Generations: Native Writers on Writing* and *From Sand Creek*.

Poets also like to write about their families of origin [understatement of the year]. While there are sibling-rivalry and sibling-bond poems, such as Jim Daniels' "Brushing my Teeth with My Sister after the Wake," I've lost count of how many poems I've read (and written) about parents (growing elderly, sadly deceased, or troublesomely alive, depending on the poets' experiences). After teaching for 20 years, trust me: parental influence is easily one of the top three themes (at least, in my poetry workshops). One of my favourite parental poems is by Sharon Olds: "I Go Back to May 1937."

I've seen moving and intricate poems about origins that weren't biological but were spiritual, geographical, immigrant- or emigrant-focused, political, or patriotic (or combinations of all categories). Walt Whitman wrote poems about Abraham Lincoln's leadership at a pivotal, devastating time in American history, and mourned his loss as if Lincoln were his own biological father in "O Captain! My Captain!"

"Here Captain! dear father!
This arm beneath your head!
It is some dream that on the deck,
You've fallen cold and dead."

Whether you explore the origins of your DNA-related ancestors, your adopted family/families and friends, cultural identities, beloved (or loathed) leaders or nemeses, or your homeland(s), **there's a long history in poetry of ancestries and heritage-themed verse just waiting for your own unique contribution (no spit vial required).**

Try this Prompt! Draft a poem addressed to an ancestor or your home community. Just because it's about the past doesn't mean it can't be snarky and/or funny.

Don't know about your family's extended history and/or don't know much about your community (then or now)? No worries: head to your local thrift shop, flea market, or even online antique site and buy one of those "instant ancestor" photos for a song. Now, you're all set. **Who do *you* think these people were? Who did *they* think they were? What do their clothes and mannerisms suggest? Who were their interlopers? What would one or more of the people in the photo say if they could whisper in your ear right now?** Write for 15 minutes. Go!

Seashell Coffee and Tea for Three: Symbolic Imagery

Last month, my darling nieces came from Missouri for a visit. After hugs and unpacking, there were presents. Out of all the new books, stuffed toys (including two lilac-haired poodles), and oodles of snazzy new clothes in neon pastels from Nana and Pappy T, their favourite plaything swiftly emerged: a long, woven basket chock-full of seashells.

The shells are nine years old—older than both nieces combined—and gathered during the last beach trip my extended family took from landlocked parts to gaze on the rolling marvels of ocean currents. Often, they sit in basement storage. My elder niece asked about them on the phone, recalling them from last year, so they were brought to a prominent spot on the porch.

How eagerly the girls, my five-year-old mini me in lavender glasses and my two-and-a-half-year-old birthday twin, ran directly to the basket after hopping out of the rental van. They raked their fingers through the fan-shaped orange pastel shapes. They held to the July light oblongs and scallops and rectilinear fragments shot through with lacy mollusc holes. Their nimble fingers set to work making a lasso-like grouping, plunking end-to-end, across the wooden boards.

One of them, the enterprising elder, noticed that the dark grey and white oyster shell (which, to my eyes, resembled a turkey foot with the characteristic toe-webbing) could double as a saucer. That meant piling another shell on top of it would make a tea or coffee cup. A rousing game of café ensued.

Immediately, Cora Vi delegated Sylvie Ro as waitress and instructed that the coffee wasn't hot enough. Sylvie Ro, ever game for anything her elder sister declares fun, rushed a shellfragment shaped like a pale-pink ridged wing atop a slate-grey oyster shell from one end of the deck to her big sister's side, the fragments clacking with each step.

I couldn't resist jumping into the imaginative game for a spell with an affected upper-crust accent for the pleasure of it.

"Oh, waitress, darling! Over here! I'd like a mint tea with honey, darling, and my friend here needs a teeny, tiny extra-hot steaming espresso. Would you like extra foam, Bitsy?"

Cora Vi, a serious look taking over her sensitive brow, swivelled her chin and said in almost a whisper, "No, Melmo. They only sell coffee at this place."

"Ah, terribly sorry, Bitsy, darling, and no extra cream it is then," I nodded, archly.

During five out of six days of their visit, the girls were absorbed in a world where seashells were serving sets. Some had crenelated, rough edges. Others were worn almost as smooth as sea glass. None of them sat in the basket for long. Who could blame them for favouring the shells over store-bought surprises? **Children, like readers, prize authenticity and can spot it from a mile away.** They understand hue, shape, and symbolism inherently and are affected by them, even if they aren't able yet to articulate how these factors influence and move them.

Try these tips for infusing imagery with symbolic meaning:

- **Choose one vivid image and stick with it for a while.** Notice in the above passage how I might have briefly mentioned other images, but how the seashells—their colours, shapes, and textures as well as the sound effects they made together—were centre stage and easily discernible as the main imagery of the piece. The seashells become symbolic of family time spent together (both years ago while gathering the shells and now while at play with the nieces). **Once you zero in on an image, consider the potential personal symbolism of that image: What are you doing with that object? What draws you to that object? How does it symbolize this stage of your life or your hopes for the next stage(s) of life? Then edit your piece—through skilful repetition of the image and/or sculpting of other, lesser images**—so that the main imagery takes centre stage.

- When choosing which image is most effective in a piece, **consider the underlying meanings of**

the object. While I have a personal connection to the shells, I am certainly not the only person I've ever known who enjoyed gathering the sea's refuse for poetic inspection. One of my favourite poets, Mary Oliver, often writes of items noticed or gathered along the seashore, and many of my friends (writers or not) have spent time with family collecting bits and pieces to take home. The thing is, though, that **shells are infused with meaning above and beyond the humans that touch them.** They represent the world of ocean currents, waves, and sea creatures that cannot speak but nonetheless communicate wholeheartedly. **The objects we collect and remember have resonance before we even touch them—why not play up those additional layers of meaning?**

- As you edit your piece, ask: **What will your readers intuit from how you've written about the object? How will it also speak to their own life experiences? Is there something you could add or take away that would create additional resonance? Especially in a piece as small as a poem, no image (nor even a word) should appear without adding to the piece as a whole. Selectively omitting can be as necessary as leaving white space in a painting.**

For additional inspiration on how a standard object or experience may hold rich shades of meaning in imagery, read excerpts of Pablo Neruda's odes, including "Ode to My Socks," available for free at Poets.org: www.poets.org/poetsorg/poem/ode-my-socks.

Try this Prompt!
Make a list of five or six items,
whether in your office, car/commute, or
home that represent you in some way. (It could
be argued that anything we notice in a landscape and any of the things we keep say something
about who we are and what we desire.)
Choose one of those items and pen a poem. Include in the poem at least three different images of the item (not necessarily in a row)
and clues as to why the object is symbolic of
a part of your life's journey. Go!

A Trip to the Woodshed: On Jazzing Up Writing Practice, Practice, Practice

It's not what you think, this woodshed. Not a small wooden structure in an East Coast town (my mind jumps straight to New England, with a scrim of orange autumnal leaves and a bracing Northern bluster). It has nothing to do with chopping, but with chops of a different sort.

This afternoon, I was reading a photography teacher's chapter in a visual-artist craft workbook. This particular photographer has been a jazz musician for years as well. He notes how, in jazz as in other art forms, one puts in numerous hours—years, really—of necessary practice and life experience to turn around and implement something new in the music once basic skills are ingrained. The "woodshed" (super cool lingo for plain, dull-as-dishwater practice, eh?) is an integral part of the artistic journey and as personal as fingerprints, which becomes background material as the artist steps out into making.

As a word nerd, I smiled to think of getting chops through the woodshed.

Then, I started to think about the seriousness of scales and accumulated playing. I lasted a grand total of one week with the trombone in sixth grade (all of the other instruments were taken when I signed up late; I really wanted the clarinet or flute). Yet, I sang in choirs for 15 years of schooling. Vocal warm-ups, such as singing ma-me-mi-mo-mu, were key before the transition to performing the sheet music.

As artists—a vast majority of the writers I know have tried their hands at numerous art forms and many still create in other media that inspire and inform their writing—we need to continue setting aside time on the regular to develop the basis of our skills, so that we can push our art outward, upward, and into new styles and content. I started to call my writing scales *writing practice* after rereading Natalie Goldberg's *Writing Down the Bones*.

Consider these six ways to stay motivated throughout years of practice.

- **Begin**—Sounds so simple, non? You'd be surprised. I've had students and clients who didn't want to begin their novels or essays until they had a faster computer or ergonomic desk chair or a cleaner house or apartment. **Don't overthink it or spend hundreds or (gasp!) thousands of dollars on your office and/or computer gizmos.** Pick a specific time of day/night and a place where you commit to your writing, day after day, even if just a half hour or less a day, over a long period of time. That's it. Spend the next 10 or 15 minutes jotting ideas about where and when you can write for 20 or so minutes each day, including an improvement or two if you want (perhaps bring a cosy pillow from another room into your office, start writing in the notebook someone gifted you for a holiday, or finally hang a favourite poster with writing quotes near your desk). Then jump in for your first day of practice. **Circumstances don't have to be perfect to practice, just conducive and personal.**

- **Create writing rituals.** Pair tea time, chocolate, a run or walk, or any other incentive with your writing practice, either as a warm-up or an after-writing reward. These rituals will become important enticements on days when you feel like doing anything *but* writing.

- **Stop mid-stream when the writing is hot, and you know exactly what you'll say next.** This is an idea I borrowed from Hemingway (and other famous writers). Some of my writing students find it works well to entice them into the next day of writing practice.

- **Artful Repetition: Make Repetition Part of the Fun.** Another photography professor assigns her students to take 250 photos of one object within two hours. The caveat: students must repeat this exercise seven days in a row with the same object. At first, students groan—*What a waste of time! I'll be taking 250 of the same photo all week long!*—but then, a funny thing happens. They start to think more creatively than ever and rise to the challenge with 250 differing variations on a theme. Consider making several drafts of the same sentence, paragraph, page, chapter, or poem within the period of an hour or two. Even better if you pick an excerpt that you feel is not your best work. Begin to tweak, mould, and shape each image or phrase with slight variations of diction, tone, and phrasing. Let your rational mind rest while your subconscious peeps out in play. Itemize the variations (aim for 10 or 20) using the bullet-point button in Word, which will automatically insert a bullet before each idea upon hitting the *enter* key. Repeat the exercise for a few days up to a week. Like a jazz riff, notice just how many exciting variations you can create on an initial idea. Many times, it's not the first, fifth, or even tenth version of an idea that's the best but the fifteenth or fiftieth.

- Perhaps the most practical and longstanding of suggestions on this list: **enlist a practice buddy of your own skill level trying to accomplish what you also want—a regular writing practice. You might meet this person at a writing workshop, an MFA program, a night class, online in a discussion board, or through an art fair or seminar, even through your kids or friends of friends ("I know somebody who's also writing poems. You guys should meet! Here's his**

email"). Agree to share work once a month, once a week, or quarterly; whatever works for your own schedules. Just knowing someone else is waiting for your next poem will work wonders for your inspiration levels. **It's also a wonderful reminder to write for a specific audience.** This month, a dear friend, C, and I are swapping a new poem we write each day. By Day 21, it's become a positive habit and a delight. Were there days it was almost impossible to get to the page due to life and career obligations that took over? You bet; we both have a few ongoing teaching assignments. It's exciting, however, to see the dedication we brought to each day, even if that meant emailing our poems past 11 pm. It's also exciting to realize the accumulation of new work that likely wouldn't have happened without the swap. We've already set up our next daily swap in six months: April, for National Poetry Writing Month. **Realize that your writing buddy is also busy; when at all possible, don't send three different pieces or multiple drafts (hey, it happens—you hit the send button and then realize what you COULD have written). Also, understand if the writer doesn't have time for the next writing challenge right away. Appreciate whatever time another author offers as a rare, precious gift.**

• **Be your own best champion.** Set a (doable) personal goal. Maybe a daily swap for a month or even a week would be too much for your schedule right now. That's understandable. Be honest about your workload and life obligations as well as the way you work best—whether with a looming deadline or with stretches of free time. Then, pick a time—even if once a week, at 3:30 am before the rest of the house wakes up for a packed day (I've had many parents who take my classes who have done this technique and written astounding amounts of prose and poetry this way).

Try this Prompt!
Give either the artful repetition exercise or the stop-in-the-middle-of-the-heat trick a try. Go!

The Name Game: Choosing a Catchy Title

"Cecelia?" he asks.

"I like it. Sassy, yet sweet. And we can shorten it to Ceci."

"I'm not wild about shortening it, though. You know people will shorten it."

"What's wrong with shortening it? I think it's cute," she says.

"Nah. What about Cali?"

"Too common. We know three Calies."

"True. Sarah?"

"Too plain. Artemis?"

"No. No way."

"But it's so pretty!"

"Artemis Cooper in third grade. She was rotten. You can't do that to your kid."

"That doesn't mean our Artemis would be rotten."

"Nope. It'll always bring to mind Artemis Cooper for me. Veto."

"How about Daphne?"

"Daphne? But you can't shorten it, unless you do Daph, which sounds weird."

"I thought you hated shortened names."

"I like nicknames; I just don't like Ceci. And Daphne sounds like the cartoon duck. Veto."

Sound familiar? A name, much like a title, is often the first impression a person presents to the world. It carries symbolic weight, hope, and background—sometimes of the chooser's culture, heritage, education, outlook, politics, religion, generation, or personal outlook. As with naming a child, the creator usually gets the honour of bestowing the moniker on their creation, for the positivity or detriment of the creation.

It may seem deceptively easy at times to slapdash a few words onto the top of the page (and I've done so myself, often as a place marker to be replaced later), but an appropriate title is your editors' and readers' first introduction to the theme and/or tone of your work. [Big breath.] That's one of the reasons why so many writers find it challenging—to say the least—to know what to call their poems.

I remember attending a one-hour seminar in grad school about the challenges of giving titles to poems—it's the kind of topic that you will encounter throughout your life as a poet, whether you decide to write solely for yourself or, more likely, share your work with loved ones or a broader literary audience during spoken-word readings and in literary journals. It's a big responsibility, but it also has potential for big creative fun.

As we venture into title-giving territory, here are some ways to instil meaningful titles that will intrigue your audience and resonate with your poems:

- **Pick a line or phrase from the poem itself.** This is my favourite method of titling my own works. Is there a particular phrase or line that your writing group complimented you on or that you enjoy each time you reread the draft? Is there a combination that underscores the protagonist or a key idea in the poem?

- **Let your title mirror your theme.** Does your poem explore a particular main idea, event, or topic? Consider the title: "On _____." Many poems have been written on the topics of love, hate, graduation, marriage, divorce, and death. You may choose to add more than one detail to the title to personalize, such as: "On Returning Home Early from the Prom in 1997" or "On Descending Mt Kilimanjaro on One Leg."

- **Place name poem name.** Some poems are set in an interesting place or time. For instance, W.H.Auden's famous poem about the start of WWII in Europe is titled with impact: "September 1, 1939." Instantly, the reader is aware not only of when this poem takes place but of a crucial historical event and milestone taking place in the poem.

- **If your poem has a protagonist or if the poem is addressed to someone in particular, name the poem after the speaker or addressee.** You might also throw in another intriguing detail or two to hook your reader, such as: "For Cole, Age 4."

- **Go against the grain. Remain open to the possibility that your title might not have much to do directly with the content of your poem, and yet ...** If the subtle approach is more your style, then this is the way to go. You might choose an intriguing word that denotes emotional or figurative content in your poem, such as: "Miasma" or "Mystique" that could mean almost anything when combined with the body of your poem and may invite your audience to make close reads.

- **Read your poem to a friend or fellow writer. What jumps out at her/him first?** That's right: borrow from those creative minds around you. Poem titles don't always have to originate with their authors. I've bounced unnamed poems off of some writing friends and family members and found that they are great at suggesting relevant titles that I never would have thought of on my own.

Conversely, what are some ideas for titling that tend to dive-bomb? Don't, repeat *don't*, do this to your readers.

- **Vague titles.** "Sister" or "A Car" don't inspire the reader into the poem; instead, they suggest whatever follows will be average and possibly melodramatic or sentimental. Readers read poems to identify with the writer's point of view, not to be reminded of how average much of life experience can be.

- **Titles that give away the poem's entire narrative.** This is especially problematic in short-form poems, like haiku and Tanka, but in any type of poem, you want to keep back some mystery so that the readers don't anticipate everything the poem will share. Otherwise, they'll stop reading midstream or, almost as bad, never return back to read or recommend the poem after the first read.

- **Titles that give away the punch line/culmination of the poem.** Similar to someone telling you the end of a book or a movie is the title that frontloads the poem's main event or conflict so that it is familiar when the reader encounters the idea again in the body of the poem. Do you like having air deflated from your tires and then riding down the street? Readers don't appreciate this buzz-kill either because much of the satisfaction of a good poem is reaching the aha! line or lines within the work.

- **The title that anyone could write in two minutes.** This one is a bit trickier to discern. Like its cousin, the vague title, it has a commonplace tone. It might also include a theme that is yawn-inducing or part of daily life so much that it makes a reader wonder why they should bother to read your poem. "School Days," "My Dad, the Hero," "My First Job," or "First Day of School." Yes, these titles may suggest theme, but they lack originality. Give readers a reason to be excited about your poem: the prospect that they are meeting an original, articulate mind; these titles don't.

Try this Prompt!
Pick three of these methods and give your poem a title based on all three. Compare and contrast, choosing the title that seems to fit your draft best.

A Green Eel
Named Yellow:
On (Suspending)
Poetic Logic

My extended family explored the National Aquarium today with my visiting nieces, who had never been. Among the stingrays, eels, tortoise, myriad schools of fish, dolphins, simulated rainforest, and ibis and other birds, there was the requisite stop at the gift shop.

Cora Vi chose the girly, carnation-pink stuffed turtle with the shiny pink shell that matched her pink-striped dress while Sylvie Ro gravitated immediately to the acid-green electric eel.

"What have you named them?" I asked, as they clutched their new stuffed toys in happy hands.

"I call mine Pink Best Friend," Cora Vi says.

"Mine Yellow," Sylvie Ro announces as she twirls the long, snake-like body around her neck and down her torso, winding it around herself like Sheena, Queen of the Jungle.

"He's green," more than one of us says.

"His name Yellow," Sylvie Ro insists, and we all smile, shake our heads a bit, and go along with it. One of my high school friends once had a yellow teddy bear named Blue.

"It was just blue to me," I recall her saying, "so I named him that at the time." Who can argue with that kind of inspiration?

In poetry, there have been entire movements influenced by logic that was topsy-turvy, seemingly random, and intriguing. The Surrealists come to mind. Such poets as André Breton, Paul Éluard, Robert Desnos, Arthur Rimbaud, Max Ernst, Guillaume Apollinaire, and Federico Garcia Lorca, wrote poems that were steeped in dream imagery and frequently in political resistance to such movements as Fascism primarily between the two World Wars. They lived in desperate, war-torn landscapes and during times where basic institutions and any sense of stability were taken from them.

The unconscious as well as images of violence and decay are frequently featured in their poems as is a technique called automatic writing, where a person free-writes without stopping to structure and without going back later to edit or formulate a logical narrative from the draft. Whatever shows up on the page of its own free will appears in the poem. As such, Surrealists juxtaposed images that are normally not blended or seen in today's reality.

Certainly, not everyone was or is a fan of such works, although many poets find them refreshing and not dissimilar from the unrest within our own times. Dream imagery can be highly personal, and political poetry is not everyone's taste. Still, **as poets we can learn much from the Surrealists' approach to drafting poems.**

- **Breaking the logic barrier can open us up to a new approach.** Ever say (or hear someone else in a workshop or class say), "But that's the way it really happened!" when someone suggests making a change, such as omitting details, compressing others, or rewriting a line or stanza for clarity? It may have happened that way, it's true, but the pacing of real life can be slow, tedious, and let's face it: boring. Many times, especially if poems are based on true events, we can get so caught up in the order of happenings that our poems bulge with unnecessary details.

- **Poetry with a strong focus on imagery, especially juxtaposed imagery, is powerful, vivid, and often succinct. Poetry thrives on compression.** Word-pictures are the best way to both interest readers and cause them to process the main themes and ideas in your work in a short space.

- The unconscious is well worth considering and even writing. **Many of our dreams—whether at night or daydreams—contain our deepest fears and questions** about ourselves, others, our culture(s), and the conundrums of living a modern life, which serve as interesting topics to explore.

- **Sharply focused, unusual imagery can be an excellent way to address big themes with resonance and without brow-beating readers or clotting drafts with clichés.** Recurring symbols, settings, people, and events might point the way to a subject you hadn't even realized you wanted to explore but that set the stage for poems that connect readers with the writer, especially given that many human fears and frustrations are similar across times and place—such as defeat, death, hope and loss of hope, and fear of failure to name a few.

- **Remember: poems mirror life, and life is frequently messy, illogical, and strange.** Invite some clashing images and discordant themes into your poems and see what happens. Jack Kerouac, Allen Ginsberg, Lawrence Ferlinghetti, Kenneth Rexroth, Diane di Prima, Gregory Corso, and the Beats often explored these themes. Frank Bidart's work also. **It can also be enjoyable to pick a stringent form, like a sonnet or senryu, and employ vibrant, expansive, or opposing images, creating a natural tension between structure and content.**

So, a green eel named Yellow? Why not?

Try this Prompt!
For a week, write down any dream
imagery you experience or can remember
upon waking. After a week, reread your notes.
Begin to mix and match recurring images and
themes to create a poem that doesn't read as true-
to-life but that illustrates important views or
lessons of life—or your interpretation of it. Don't
(over)explain—set discordant or strange
images and symbols next to each other.
For inspiration, I've included two dream
poems I've written using this process.

"Ovum Dream"
For CB: friend, fellow writer, dream interpreter extraordinaire

I fissured the shells open,
exposing a magic act—
gushing moons, buttery discs,
from pastel Styrofoam
ruptured

one at a time. But from one ivory encasing
a ribbon of four yolks flowed, full-sized—
three of the yolks bright black,
inky eclipses. I did not marvel at this
multiplication,

this bounty from one enclosure. My worry:
to whirl together what was given
or pitch them and begin again?
I did not wear an apron, I was all hands
razzmatazzing runny fluid into a crock.
The black yolks suspended orbs,
beautiful dark buoyancy in the glass chamber.

Were these ova the obvious—physical fertility
for a woman without children, creativity,
transmutation from hunger?
Or that I'd made a scrambled
sandwich hours before turning in?

In this vision, questioning myself on
what to do: I kept cracking them open,
the kitchen counter slick with sunny morning.
To whisk or to toss not the question at all;
I did nothing but the one trick
I knew. Rift and spill, rift and spill.
Waking to continue on paper.

"En Route"

All the rooms were painted goldenrod,
      one after one after one,
and the buffet had many fruits whose names
      the Australians in line behind me
kept explaining to my clueless cohorts.

The dress I was wearing when I looked down
      a jungle green with jade and red
birds, the flounce of the skirt pretty and full.
      I was pleased. Everyone else
in khaki and a t-shirt. You would spot me

across the crowd. The beautiful petite woman
      scooping eggs. Where'd she come from? Your lover
I sensed. I still found the blue rubber-band at my nape,
      shook my hair loose. The china of the plate
so ivory my face almost disappeared on its surface.

Everything I've Got Belongs to You:
On Tone

"I WISH OUR CLEVER YOUNG POETS WOULD REMEMBER MY HOMELY DEFINITIONS OF PROSE AND POETRY; THAT IS, PROSE—WORDS IN THEIR BEST ORDER; POETRY—THE BEST WORDS IN THEIR BEST ORDER." — SAMUEL COLERIDGE TAYLOR

When it comes to instantly recognizable tone, Blossom Dearie should get a prize. If you've never heard the singer (incredibly, it's not a stage name), you're in for a treat. Her voice is incandescent as carbonation bubbles in a curved glass and a cross between Bettie Boop, Marilyn Monroe, and an all-her-own pleasant burble. There's a kittenish, coy note to it, but also wisdom without playing the cynic—a difficult balance to manage without singing chops. While her repertoire is decidedly old-school jazz standards from the 1940s-1960s and she passed away in 2009, much of her catalogue is available online for all generations to enjoy thanks to the wondrous interwebs.

In my twenties, a friend with a staggeringly diverse record collection and an even bigger knowledge of music history included one of Dearie's songs on a mix cd—ahh, remember those clever Valentines?—and my first thought was: "Hey, that's the Schoolhouse Rock lady!" If you're Gen X like I am, you'll recognize her kewpie-doll songs from grammar videos brought to you by an elementary school near you on a clunky VCR-TV combo as big as an oven. Whether it's jamming about the jive of conjunctions and proper nouns that need capitalization or teasing harmoniously on "Everything I've Got Belongs to You" and "I Won't Dance," there's a quality to her light, sweet soprano that's instantly good-moodable. Don't we all need more of those? That she could be instructive to six-year-olds, captivating to couples, and commiserative with glum adults speaks well of her audience range.

Similarly, some poets, including Denise Levertov, Mark Doty, Jack Gilbert, Adrienne Rich, Lucille Clifton, David Mura, and Quenton Baker, have a tone that is instantly recognizable and distinctive.

As writers, our tone should also be recognizable and part of our style. What are some methods to identify our tone and cohere to it?

- **Pay attention to syntax.** How do you combine words for maximum impact? If you're writing formal verse with a rhyme pattern, some of the ends of your lines may be impacted by the form's requirement. Conversely, whether formal or free-verse, look to see how you combine words. For instance, do you frequently use alliteration to create a melodious tone?

- **Do you use formal or informal diction/word choices?** We poets are particular about shades of meaning. Writing "overcoat" gives a different, more formal feeling than plain-old, working-class "jacket." Readers come to inhabit the emotions and world you've set up for them via subtle nuances of meaning.

- **Notice punctuation patterns.** Are you the kind of author who punctuates periodically, with long lines and even longer stanzas such as Walt Whitman? Or do you prefer more staccato sentences and frequent commas and dashes like Emily Dickinson? Or, do you hardly use any punctuation at all à la e.e. cummings? Or, might you use a single stanza without breaks or wrap-around text, as in prose poems?

- **Do you have recurring subject matter/themes?** Do your poems cover repeated subjects or linked narrative territory? Some poets write about inanimate objects while other poets are well-known for writing deeply personal, Confessional works about their own lives. Other poets write about their children or parents, their jobs, the death of loved ones, their rollercoaster love lives, or a particular event or time period—whether historical or broader, such as college or being a young adult. Over and over again.

- **What kinds of titles do you choose for your poems?** Although it may seem subtle, titles are the first impression your poems make in the world. The titles you choose set the tone for what follows. Make sure the text and the title match and do so without giving away too much of the poem; instead, invite the readers into your work. Are your titles succinct and broad, such as "The Birthday," or long and lyric with multiple clauses?

Try this Prompt!

Pull up several drafts of recent poems and look for the five markers of tone noted above. Highlight each one with a different colour to spot them more effectively, and then note your tone patterns. **How might you strengthen your tone by adhering more to your natural style? Consider including more of what you have the least of currently.** If you need help identifying markers of your style, swap work with a writing friend or accountability partner—it's often easier for someone else to point out patterns in work, and we can return the favour for another willing artist.

The Turkey from Albuquerque: On Scope and Setting in Writing

Today is Thanksgiving Eve eve. Besides the epic grocery-store trip (which I finished yesterday with a precariously piled cart, whew) and the baking ahead (hello, apple crisp later today and gingerbread tomorrow), there are other delicious offerings in store.

My sister has called on the way to her own food forage to say that my elder niece's program at school went well this morning. My brother-in-law just uploaded the clip of Cora Vi, with a burgundy sweater, dark skirt, and pink glitter sneakers I'd like to nab for my own closet, on stage with 20 other kindergarteners.

My sister tells me that my niece was beyond thrilled yesterday, saying: "Mama, I can sing all my songs for you!" and then she launched into an excited, impromptu living-room rehearsal on the worn tan-suede sofa.

It shows: How proud she is to wear her construction-paper turkey headdress, with dangling feather-shaped appendages in orange, brown, and red splaying in three different directions and bouncing from her curls like water in a fountain! How delighted her smile as she shyly looks into the crowd, as her sneakers come to a screeching halt, as her hands hold each other, and she sways her white-tights-clad knees next to the deathly pale girl with ebony hair who is a dead ringer for a student of mine from years ago. I do the quick mental math: that student I met as a child is now a freshman in college.

As I watch, a few things hit me: Cora Vi knows all of the words by heart. My smart elder niece! Her eye contact and vocal form are laudable, too. Also, although I've never set foot in this particular school, I can almost smell the wafts that emanate from the wooden-floor stage: shoe polish, lemon-dunked industrial cleaner, and overexcited, twitchy-with-energy bodies. I can feel the unexpected hit of heat from the auditorium lights prickling my crown (a featherless- paper crown, but still).

I have no idea the words to this poem about the bird from New Mexico, sung to "Oh, my Darling Clementine" (a ditty my elementary school music teacher—who was also a dear friend's mom— taught my class), but I almost find myself swaying and bopping as I hear every third word the students mumble with marble-mouthed gusto. Their brown-paper-bag vests coloured over with crayon markings to approximate turkey flesh make a body want to gobble-gobble as the herky-jerky turkeys make the assembled parents on fold-down chairs clap and smile while holding camera phones aloft.

The words, anyway, are beside the point in this instance—something I so rarely say about anything.

I feel a surge of missing my nieces combined with affection as I realize that my elder niece—whom I haven't seen in four months since we live 18 hours apart—has grown lankier and taller (like her parents) in our physical absence and, at the same time, her facial features look even more like my younger self—chin indentation, glasses, and all. (The angelic spiral curls are still a gift from her mother and father.)

I begin to think about the layers of life that a writer can tap into and use to enrich verse.

I sang in school choirs for many years, was in National Honor Society as a high schooler, had a minor role in a youth-group play my junior year (it was only two or three pages of dialogue, but I had such a tough time remembering my lines that sometimes, I still have the anxiety dream where I haven't practiced and yet am onstage performing and making up nonsense lines that I know are bombing based on my fellow actors' mean glares), and participated in many other school activities involving stages and gyms. There's something about that odd combination of nerves, anticipation, and stage polish that reeks in my memory of cleaning chemicals, overhead-light blindness while still trying to scope the seats for familiar faces, and joyous amazement that the moment to perform has arrived. No more rehearsal! **It's paradoxically one of those moments where you are most in your body while feeling out of body at the same time.** As an introvert, solos made my knees feel like knocking, but there was something particularly fulfilling about the waft of four-part harmony rising to the exposed rafters as a single, solid wall of sound and the relief valve of exiting the risers at the finale.

Inside, I still carry the sense impressions of those spaces as well as those events and ceremonies, even though they are long-ago relics of my 1980s and 1990s. **Now, stages will be the realm of my young nieces, and I happily forfeit them the majority of the time. I am an auntie now, with stacks and stacks of the past that could become poetry, with stacks and stacks of poetically possible memories yet to make.**

Whatever our life roles and experiences—from parent or parental figure to performer, from boss to low-on-the-rung beginner, we all have a rich ratatouille of remembrances that we can call to mind and mix on the page. I have been the performing student, I have been the supportive friend, I have been the supportive audience/family member, and with a few details on a page I may be so again at any time as I carry these experiences and sift through them.

On my third time watching the performance, I hear my brother-in-law quietly complimenting someone in the background audio (the teacher? a class mother or administrator?) on organizing the special ceremony as the kids go to the stage.

The complimentee whispers, "Thank you. It's stressful." Her voice emphasizes the "stressful" part. Then, they laugh politely in understanding as the 20 kindergarteners take the stage by storm.

Dictionary.com describes *scope* in its noun form as "extent or range of view, outlook, application, operation, effectiveness" as well as "space for movement or activity; opportunity for operation." In its verb form, we have the slang "scope out," which offers "to look at or over; examine; check-out; to master; to figure out." **Part of the beauty of writing is the opportunity to figure out below-the-surface meanings, often in the process of reflection and drafting and then again in revision.**

When we attend plays or ceremonies, whether from the magical miracle of technology or in the hard, collapsible seats, we flash back to memories we likely have left behind, suppressed, or forgotten. **In the seats, we are still on stage. On stage, we were looking through the great glare for familiar faces in the seats. There's a symmetry and symbiotic relationship that is fulfilling and perfect for poetry.**

Let's tap into this scope to enrich our writing.

- **Combine elements of a particular place and time, as I do with my imagery of stages I've experienced. Consider all of the senses, not just our most-commonly recorded one, sight.**

- **Compare and contrast what you recall to what another generation experienced or will one day experience. What has changed since your days in the spotlight?** I recall my choir director, a Baby Boomer, choosing many pop-song arrangements from the early-to-mid-1960s (such as the Chiffons' "Sweet Talkin' Guy," which I still know by heart, and Beatles' songs) for us to perform in the early 1990s, songs I'm fairly certain high-school choirs now don't cover along with their Handel and Britten. **What seems the same? Think of a detail that was utterly unique to your place. Think of another detail that is universal.**

- Give yourself 15 or 20 minutes to do a free-write and list as many images related to a specific setting as you can recall. If dialogue snippets or conversations arise, add those to the list as potentially valuable material for later use. When you draft, consult this list and include at least two or three of the images and/or dialogue. Consider composing new work today or another day for some of the unused gold you've accumulated.

- Ask long-time friends or relatives what they remember of a certain place or event. Keep a notepad or recording device handy to record some of their responses or, better yet, make a mini movie or video clip on your phone to capture their expressions, tone of voice, and what makes them amused or uncomfortable. Be prepared to hear a completely different, perhaps refreshing or perhaps consternating series of reflections that may conflict with your own memories. Write from the rich ground of how each person recalls highly personal, idiosyncratic details. A reminder: memories aren't 100% accurate for anyone.

Try this Prompt!
Choose one of the four methods
above and then write a poem based
on a personal experience you or a loved one
had years ago. It may be as monumental and
singular as a graduation or becoming a parent
or as yearly as band concerts, military moves,
and homecoming dances. Make sure to develop
the setting for this event so that readers can envision the scene (and by extension, similar places
or times they've known). You don't have to
be the poem's speaker, but you certainly
might be. Or you may craft a character that,
whether from the stage or off, has a
lot to say or do about this particular
place. Go!

The Great American Eclipse: Commemorating Momentous Events in Poetry

As I write this, something spectacular is happening. Sun and moon overlap directly in Earth's view for mere minutes. The epicentre begins in Madras, Oregon, then travels to Casper, Wyoming and Alliance, Nebraska (where 100,000 people surround "Car Henge" in the middle of a field that is now a tourist attraction—not a hotel room in over 150 miles, thanks to the quirky event), swathing through Illinois, glimpsing through Kelly, Kentucky and Nashville to end near Columbia, South Carolina before sailing out to the oceans. 99 years ago was our last U.S. coast-to-coast full eclipse. This afternoon, we can see the corona of the sun with our naked eyes.

Only 76-79% of the sun will be covered in the Mid-

Atlantic, compared to 100% in Madras, Oregon, which is why my tiny dot on a map is traffic-congestion free but little Madras has been inundated. Here on the East Coast, there's an hour and 12 minutes until it happens, but reporters across the country are already broadcasting in fields with makeshift tent cities where everyone from students to great-grandparents from all over the nation and world have gathered.

What I savour about the eclipse hoopla: instead of fashions scions and filthy-rich reality stars, today's media glare features several NASA guest correspondents, astrophysicists, and the geeky yet loveable popular TV scientist of my youth, Bill Nye the Science Guy. My kind of event.

Some local schools have closed their doors today, afraid students' eyes will be affected if they forget and directly gaze into the sun/moon combo. On TV, while many have special glasses, many others don't—not heeding the ominous warnings that burnt retinas are like permanently gazing through murky jelly. My eyesight is bad enough for me to say no thanks to that. I'll be sitting at my desk when the amazing event happens in my own backyard, parting the curtains to look-see out as I do now—so far, so sunny.

Due to the veritable media circus online and off, I now know that the last time a complete solar eclipse happened solely in the US was 1776. It moves over four times faster than a commercial jet. I've added vocabulary of scientists: including *the diamond ring* (not of the bling variety) and *Baily's beads*.

I watch, more deeply touched than anticipated. One

woman celebrates her 78th birthday on a lawn chair, gazing upward and murmuring into a portable microphone: "I've never seen anything like it." One guy prepares to pop the question while the news channel cuts to a Midwestern wedding in St Joseph, Missouri, where a bride just exchanged her vows under an awning so that during the eclipse, her wedding reception will stop to take in the eclipse—we watch them gape up in wonder. College students and families on blankets beside them gab away to the on-scene reporters, their babies wearing the hokey-looking cardboard glasses.

I've watched three complete, televised eclipses from the American West so far—from "we have just minutes until the big event" to "it's unbelievably surreal, a sight most are seeing for the first time" to "afternoon sunlight has reappeared here. We're watching history. Amazing, just amazing." There are lots of *amazings*. Lots of *coronas* and *totalities*. The 1980's song, "Total Eclipse of the Sun," is blasting now at the televised wedding reception. Apparently, for a moment's blip, it's again a number-one song, but that—like the eclipse's brief one-to-two-minute appearance—will also pass swiftly.

One announcer used the word *primal* about his experience of the eclipse. **What is it about sky-watching?** It's instinctive and true: this tilting of the neck to gaze up. Our ancestors did it (centuries before us). Is it the same thing as exploring the vast ocean—something immense and totally outside of our power to control—something rare enough and powerful enough to injure man but also to razzle-dazzle us in the middle of a jaded, all-news-all-the-time era? Is it that we are reminded not only of time's passage but also of our place in momentous communal events? Humans are impacted by reminders that we are small, that life is unrestrained.

More than that, we like a reason to gather. Apart from online, a sense of community is often rare and precious. We live most of our 21st century attached to keyboards, individually typing into the ether, even when sitting side-by-side. People are physically and personally travelling hundreds of miles for this thing. To physically talk to fellow science-absorbed strangers in person. Science has become popular and collective; that is no small thing.

The eclipse coverage has a refreshing innocence. For Gen Xers like myself, it recalls the flavour of the early-to-mid-1980s space shuttle launches before the Challenger explosion. It also reminds me of the hubbub about Halley's Comet in 1986, when neighbour friends, my sister, and I camped out in pup tents in the back yard during the week of the county fair.

As an astute student noted when we talked about the eclipse and its meaning (or lack thereof): **"Sure, it will get dark for a while and then, it will get bright again." Exactly. That can be said for almost any large-scale event, which makes writing about milestones—both national and profoundly personal—perfect fodder for poems.**

Consider the momentous and rare events in your own life. Some events might be large-scale, affecting your community, country, or even the world. Where were you when the clock struck midnight, ushering in the new millennium in 2000? When Kennedy was shot? What were you doing on 9/11? Other events may be highly individual. What was your high-school graduation like? What happened during your first year of college or your first day of your so-called dream job? The day a loved one died? Or the day you met the love of your life? Or lost them? What were you doing and thinking on your wedding day or your divorce day?

Momentous occasions demand the best and worst from us: from heightened emotions to heightened observation, time seems to slow and then realign. They highlight our weaknesses and strengths and subconscious desires that don't always show.

For two holiday poems, check out "Earth Day on the Bay" by Gary Soto and "Taking down the Tree" by Jane Kenyon. The customs described in these poems capture both community zeitgeist and the personal feelings associated with special occasions and their aftermaths. Poems centred on celebrations, emotional baggage, and hopes frequently intermingle.

Depending on the tone you use, your readers will intuit whether the event left you feeling more connected to others or whether it alienated and made you more of an individual. Ralph Waldo Emerson's historical poem was sung at the completion of the Battle Monument, July 4, 1837, in honour of 1775's Battle of Concord, one of the first two armed conflicts in the Revolutionary War that American colonists fought against the British. For that occasion, it employs rhymes and evocative diction choices, like "foe," "Time" (with a capital), and "Spirit" (similarly capitalized) to suggest unrelenting patriotism and pride (with its formal, rhyming structure) in the midst of wartime struggle and the sacrifice of a fledgling country ("votive stone" certainly resembles a tomb stone).

"Concord Hymn"

By the rude bridge that arched the flood,
Their flag to April's breeze unfurled,
Here once the embattled farmers stood,
And fired the shot heard round the world.

The foe long since in silence slept;
Alike the conqueror silent sleeps;
And Time the ruined bridge has swept
Down the dark stream which seaward creeps.

On this green bank, by this soft stream,
We set to-day a votive stone;
That memory may their deed redeem,
When, like our sires, our sons are gone.

Spirit, that made those heroes dare,
To die, and leave their children free,
Bid Time and Nature gently spare
The shaft we raise to them and thee.

Such poems of commemoration tend to focus far less on individual wants, needs, and thoughts, and more on a community at large. After the 9/11 terrorist attacks in the US, many poets wrote about the tragedy. Commemoration or collective-ceremony is part of these poems' purpose, as are poems written for weddings, birthdays, funerals, personal and work anniversaries, and other gathering-in works.

However, momentous occasions certainly don't have to have international or national scope to be worthy of poetic treatment. Before my elder niece was born, I wrote a series of poems commemorating my excitement, anticipation, and wonder at the preparation process for welcoming a niece and for becoming an auntie. Four of the poems, including the poem below, were published as part of *Origami Poems Project* in a micro-chap called *About this World* in 2011,. *www. origamipoems.com/poets/94-melanie-faith* "newfoundling"

You are yet in the bread cave,
the woman cage whose jaws
will unhinge for passage—

what should I say, supple firecracker,
animate sapling,
about this world-place? Today there's
intermittent

thunderboomers. Driving gales. The
kind that sideways blind,
dampens hems and soddens coat-sleeves.
This, too, happens: we must meet and heft
discomfort

deepening in the marrow. Seldom, though,
does it last longer than a shiver
and a cast off,
just as your mother knits and purls,
preparing midst sickness.

When writing poems of occasion, **dig deeper, to the nooks and crannies of specific details that ring poetic and true** instead of straight reportage. My poem's first stanza includes metaphors and images of physical birth, while my second stanza applies two tender nicknames, "supple firecracker" and "animate sapling," to denote the uncontrollable essence of new creation (whether a child or a project) as well as familial connection (what is a sapling if not a young [family] tree?). The knitting metaphor ties together my sister's gestation period with her avid knitting skills along with generational ties. **Write about what you felt and said or didn't say but wanted—strived—to.** What are the stereotypes of the event and the event's preparation? Who criticized the event? Who secretly liked it? How did you feel during an event that was completely beyond your control—did you like the rush, feel humbled, upset, afraid, or a combination of something else? How did those emotions lead to actions or conversation? **When we write about our specific experience, an amazing thing often happens—our singular experience starts to become universal.**

Especially focus a spotlight on discovery and what you hadn't anticipated or that surprised you, as these reflections carry deep meaning to which your readers will connect.

My Votes for Top Six Surprise Endings (hey, it's hard to narrow down to just five!):

- "Friendship after Love" by Ella Wheeler Wilcox

- "The Writer" by Richard Wilbur

- "Summer in a Small Town" by Linda Gregg

- "Tonight No Poetry will Serve" by Adrienne Rich

- "If you want what visible reality/can give" by Rumi (translated by Coleman Barks)

- "Seven Months Later" by Meghan O'Rourke

Try this Prompt!

Make a top-10 event list. Include both national/international events that crowds of people enjoyed or experienced as well as highly personal, just-you events. Pick one national event and one personal event. Jot images related to each of the events. List external signs of celebration, disbelief, or grief. Consider not only visual images, but sound, taste, and other images as well. What snippets of conversation or wise words do you remember from those events? Jot those, too. Now, write a poem based on each of these events, including those snippets of dialogue and sensory impressions. What was stunning about the event? Include those details, too. Go! When finished, compare both drafts. Which poem is more evocative: the poem about the communal or the personal? What might you include—or even omit—to make the other poem resonate more? How might you combine a national event with a personal one? Edit accordingly.

Bonus Prompt!
Keep a running list of poems whose last line or two surprises you. Note the last line(s) in your entry, along with the title and the author. Then, study the line(s) to pinpoint specific words, phrases, imagery, or syntax that led to this surprise.

The Before-and-After Poem

I had another birthday this week. There was ice-cream cake (yum, chocolate!), Skyping with my birthday-twin niece (hello, Darling Miss Three!), and digital well-wishes of my four decades from friends across the world and from numerous scenes. I ran errands and did some teacher paperwork in the morning, was treated to lunch, and then took the afternoon and evening off to read a book, write a short story, edit a poem-in-progress, watch deliciously mindless TV, and to enjoy the once-a-year phone-call-to-end-all-phone-calls from my busy college best friend which has become one of my favourite presents. As birthdays go, it was an introvert's paradise: low-key, rejuvenating, and just about perfect. Much better than last year, when I had cold chills and a stomach virus and stayed shivering in bed all day.

As a child, I didn't always like a December birthday. It tended to take forever (*4-eva*, in child's parlance on notes passed on lined notebook paper) to get here and then was over in an eye-blink, a long-awaited blip in the hubbub of holidays. These days, I enjoy the sense of anticipation in December along with the decorations while not minding at all a few hours in the midst of the bustle to catch my breath and to celebrate another trip around the sun, daydreaming and planning for the New Year that's just a calendar flip away.

Were there people I'd have liked to have heard from but didn't? Sure. A friend of mine comes to mind. The last time we saw each other three years ago, the final thing I said after catching up on our creative ventures, hugging, and wishing each other well on the sidewalk, reluctant to part as people passed in the bracing wind, bundled in coats and gloves in early evening darkness, was: "I'm headed this way" as I pointed to the left. He was parked in another lot in the opposite direction. I remember a kind of hyper-alert sounding in my mind that felt cellular (the same part of my brain that records and recognizes events as important to write about); *we're not just heading in separate directions for an evening*. Our jobs, our lives were veering onto two paths that would take us apart for who-knew-how-many years. It was a moment that divided our friendship from the close-proximity years to the barely-hear-from-you era. Beyond ego, I knew it was the right thing; we both had new projects we were excited about, and he had adventures and changes ahead. Of course, that didn't mean I relished it. This is a feeling many writers likely resonate with, in this era of adjuncts, freelancers, and economic and job insecurity that sees many creatives enter the arts with enthusiasm and determination and then proceed to keep many balls in the air with big hearts but less energy and flagging enthusiasm. Employers assign more and more work for the same salary, jobs dry up or fall through, and there are more applicants for less and less funding year after year. Our intuition—about changing relationships as well as how much upheaval we can stand in our working conditions—proves a powerful touchstone in our increasingly disjunctive lives.

As poets, we pay attention to this kind of before-and-after experience with concentration that most people are too busy running here-and-there to notice. We divide time into a personal and profound series of images. Here are some ways poets explore then-and-now.

- **Things were rolling along swimmingly … until, abruptly, they weren't. Poems can shine a light on that halting transition from fine to never-the-same.** Perhaps it's a personal tragedy (an accident or assault, a death in the family, divorce, being fired or jobless), but it can also be group suffering (terrorist attacks, school shootings, domestic violence, discrimination, homelessness).

- **The Milestone.** Birthdays, reunions, anniversaries, promotions. It's the large event that divides then from now. It could be a celebration that's part of your culture—the bar or bat mitzvah, first communion, wedding, or graduation—or it could be more private and personal than that. These events trigger comparison and contrast, between our younger selves and our current or future selves . They might also be quarterly or yearly recurring events, and yet, something within us has changed and is worth commemorating.

- **The Start-over.** Perhaps you've moved, gone into remission, or recently lost weight. At times of transition, poetry provides a way to process complicated situations, people, and emotions. **Hope and healing aren't a straight-to-the-top, one-stop trajectory, and our art form can reflect that truth.** There are starts, stops, redoes, and retries that are meaningful themes for verse.

- **Changes in the environment and/or natural world. It's not just people that experience dramatic adjustment and transformation; places also undergo overhauls through time.** The park where you rode bikes and played as a kid might now be a super store or business suite with a paved parking lot. Conversely, there might be a new community garden where you enjoy getting your fingernails dirty in earth as the seedlings you plant take root and yield produce or petals. Nature poets have long celebrated landscapes with awe and wonder and open eyes to the turbulence within the natural world, from Mary Oliver to Camille Dungy, from the haiku poets of ancient Japan (Basho, Buson, and Issa, I'm looking at you!) to Keats, Coleridge, and Shelley to the Transcendentalists in New England and Romantics in the 1800s (greetings, Emerson and Thoreau; fare well, William Cullen Bryant), to Robert Frost and Wendell Berry in more-recent times.

Try this Prompt!
Jot down two or three ideas from your own life (or someone else's) for each of the four before-and-after categories. Then, pick one for today's free-write. Repeat this exercise until you've either explored your entire list or have new before-and-after poem ideas to follow. For fun and further inspiration, go to www.poetryfoundation.org and peruse poems by some of the nature poets listed above.

On Pear Photography and Seasonal Poetry

It's that time of year again: **I spent 20 minutes this afternoon photographing pears.** First, I snapped one solitary and sumptuous fruit and its reflection against mottled stone, then groupings of three and four, then, noticing nearby lacy reflections from a wispy, bug-eaten rose-bush branch, I experimented with combining leaf-reflections and fruit.

Each pear, dappled with freckles and speckles, is utterly unique as a fingerprint. In tones from golden tan to celery green and with pinprick mottles in tans, taupes, and sepias, whether they have stems or not is beside the point as are the variations of shape—each is magnificent as-is, even with indentations and dings from hail or rain. The heft of one in the palm is a spherical softball but daintier. Once ripe, the taste of the Bartletts is soft yet fragrant as eau de cologne. **They are symbols of anticipation and early harvest fulfilment.**

Their mid-to-late August appearance on the table means another milestone of seasonal change is right around the corner: the fall semester. And with it, another favourite of mine: stationery-shopping season.

Oh, the enticements of new notebooks with their blue-ruled pristine pages carrying the whiff of ideas-to-come, the colourful and clickable pencils and pens awaiting the desk cup, the staples seeking the click-click-click of recently churned drafts in all of their glorious and hopeful imperfection! It's a wonder I make it out of the store without buying the whole aisle.

In fashion-speak, **this is a transitional time for our minds *and* closets** with women's magazines suggesting how to cling to short-sleeved dresses and skirts longer by introducing fall separates like multicolour tights in shades of oxblood and goldenrod and draping the infamously cute cardigan over bare shoulders.

Just two more weeks until Labour Day, that slightly sad-tinged final picnic hurrah, where Americans bid bye-bye to sweet summer sunlight.

Poets have long been concerned with savouring each step of the season we're in as well as looking to those moments of transitioning into the next phrase. The overlapping of weather conditions (external signs of the season) with accompanying internal changes is a particularly effective way to express time's passage in a meaningful way.

Keats' poem, "The Human Seasons" takes the reader through all four seasons in the span of a jaunty, metrical sonnet.

"The Human Seasons"

Four Seasons fill the measure of the year;
There are four seasons in the mind of man:
He has his lusty Spring, when fancy clear
Takes in all beauty with an easy span:
He has his Summer, when luxuriously
Spring's honied cud of youthful thought he loves
To ruminate, and by such dreaming high
Is nearest unto heaven: quiet coves
His soul has in its Autumn, when his wings
He furleth close; contented so to look
On mists in idleness—to let fair things
Pass by unheeded as a threshold brook.
He has his Winter too of pale misfeature,
Or else he would forego his mortal nature.

But why should fall get all the glory? There are classic cavortings through flowers, robins, and all things lovey-dovey in works such as fanciful all-over-the-page popper "[in Just-]" by e.e.cummings and "When Lilacs Last in the Dooryard Bloom'd" for my fellow Whitman-aholics. The third section is my favourite and as exquisite description of at-last-spring landscapes as any I've had the joy to experience:

"3"
In the dooryard fronting an old farm-house near the white-wash'd palings,
Stands the lilac-bush tall-growing with heart-shaped leaves of rich green,
With many a pointed blossom rising delicate, with the perfume strong I love,
With every leaf a miracle—and from this bush in the dooryard,
With delicate-color'd blossoms and heart-shaped leaves of rich green,
A sprig with its flower I break.

And let's not forget a profusion of perfectly bite-size haiku, tanka, and haibun (haiku/prose combos) in celebration of all seasons and directly incorporating seasonal words, such as this playful favourite by Issa:

Face of the spring moon—
about twelve years old,
I'd say.

When does the new year begin for you? What are the signs and harbingers of a fresh season set to begin in your world? As a lifelong student and teacher for 20 years, my internal clock is set to turn over on the first day of class each fall.

Try this Prompt!
Read a few of these seasonal poems or research some on your own. Pick a season and write an allusion in your poem to one of the poems you read, as MacLeish does. Your poem should take place and/or focus on the season, yes, but (as with the above examples) it should also explore something deeper and more personal about the human condition, time's passage, and your intimates. Go!

Three-Sided Seed: Adventures in Poetic Closure

Yesterday, I wrote a poem about the seed I found a week ago. Unlike most seeds, which are as perfectly spherical as unpopped popcorn, this one had three distinct sides. Still, it's the kind of tiny, commonplace object that could easily get overlooked (and usually does) in the daily rush. It's the kind of small piece of almost-trash that could drop from a pocket or a drawer and get swept away with a crunch on a shoe-bottom or the suction-nozzle of the vacuum. But it doesn't—it didn't this time.

"Three-Sided Seed"

Kept in a palm
after a nature walk,
I forget

which plant
it originates from.
Perfect

in its crookedness,
sides like seams,
like a metal toy jack.

Tawny and
smooth, its hardness
a kept kernel

I like to trace and twirl
in the deep
right pocket

of my green silk jacket,
my nature-made
fidget spinner.

This seed
will not sprout petals.
This tripod seed has its own

purpose.
Sense memory of an unpaved
path;

it carries
within the core: sunlight,
tolerable patience.

Poetic starts can seem endlessly easy at times. Sparks of inspiration from noticing something anew happen just about anywhere. The harder part, at least for me and many of my poetry-writing students, occurs from the mid-stream to the end. Especially the end. **A new idea launches us only so far, and then what?**

Endings are integral—especially the last lines, where your reader will take away the final kernels you've left for them. We shouldn't settle for the almost-right lines. Up to the end, we must experiment, we must push through until the ending that the poem (and the reader) needs is in place.

Tips for poetic closure:

- **An ending is a chance to highlight a theme or push the theme into surprising territory.** The draft of my poem above is a third draft. In the first draft, the original last stanza was:

"It carries
within the core:
sunlight soft and clean as pine boughs."

- **Yet that ending didn't resonate, it didn't take the poem further or push the idea of the seed into any kind of framework beyond the literal surroundings of the seed when I found it.** The idea that the seed was a symbol of patience arrived with the second draft and made the seed's symbolism richer.

- **Consider closing on an abiding image that will stick with the reader long after the poem's end.** In my final stanza, two images are planted (pardon the pun): sunlight and a core. Most readers will envision yellow rays and the centre of a seed when they read those lines. While the core is a bit amorphous, it pairs well with the similarly shapeless virtue of patience.

- **Cut any redundancy or clutter. Often, when composing, we're unsure of where the poem wants to end, so we just keep going, piling up line after line in a stab at finding the one that fits best. While this is okay in a first draft, edit out many of these lines from your poem in later drafts**—they are place-markers and frequently cover no new or interesting territory. My second draft of my poem ended:

"It carries
within the core: sunlight,
voiceless patience in wait."

I omitted the pine boughs from a nearby tree. Since the seed wasn't a cone and didn't come from the pine, they were beside the point. I'd moved the sunlight to the previous (middle) line, creating a stage for that final line to perform. As I sat with the poem for a few more hours after teaching and cleaning, it occurred to me that the poem was about the persistence that the seed contained.

In went the word "patience." Also, into the third line went the word "voiceless." My initial plan was to suggest silence, the kind of deep silence that we feel in nature but also while being forced to wait on someone else and their (sometimes glacial) timing. Since this seed wasn't going to be flowering in my pocket, as I suggest, I felt the inertness of "voiceless" might be a match. So, in went the prepositional phrase "in wait." This is a seed waiting to bloom that never will. It made sense literally but, again, poetically it felt redundant. Didn't "patience" often imply waiting, anyway? "In wait" also felt slightly awkward next to the word "patience." Backspace-backspace-backspace. After checking my email and writing myself a note, I returned to the draft again and also backspaced "voiceless," as it kept niggling at me as something that stuck out like a sore thumb, the kind of word that is more about humans than nature and so would pull the reader out of the poem's subtle, twist ending.

- **Resonance jars us out of stale expectations. Left hooks aren't just for the boxing ring. Final stanzas often lead us where we expect and then veer into new territory that deepens the initial experience.** In the case of my poem, the final stanza retains the expected image of sunlight and then ends with a word that tumbled through my mind again and again: "tolerable." Sure, we're told all of our lives to be patient, but how often do we find patience acceptable? Pretty much never. Exercising patience or, worse, being admonished to have some patience is painful, frustrating, and blood-pressure raising. Yet, the more I thought about it, the more those specific two diction choices "tolerable patience" next to each other offered refreshing meaning to the last line—and a take-away that made narrative sense and gave a deeper, spiritual quality to the poem.

"it carries
within the core: sunlight,
tolerable patience."

On one hand, this is a poem about a physical seed. On the other hand—and with the pairing of a human stumbling block—it has become about more than just nature. The poem's engine runs because of its theme: forbearance. Readers the world over experience the daily need to harness patience on multiple levels and must find reserves within (or without, as with the possession of this seed) to make something unpleasant "tolerable."

- **Even if you're writing about something that actually happened, the ending doesn't have to be bound by fact. Quite the opposite.** My jacket isn't silk (just green). I don't know what's inside of the seed (I'd have to smash it open to see, and I like it too much for that), and I'm sure it doesn't contain a literal representation of the physical "patience" I personify it to have. Does any of that matter to the meaning of the poem? Nope. **In poetic endings, feel free to make imaginative leaps and to omit certain information that doesn't leave the reader with a take-away. Your poem will still be authentic.** Sure, there was an inspiration point, but the ending must serve the poem (and the readers of the poem).

- **Consider circling back.** This particular poem didn't use this technique, but I've employed it in many of my drafts and seen it work well in other poets' pieces, too. **Your opening lines might contain an image or phrase that can be artfully repeated at the ending, now that the reader has a deeper understanding of your theme, setting, characters, and/or narrative.** Such purposeful repetition can be used to great effect in the final stanza and, often, **in the final line as a sort of refrain that creates symmetry as well as deeper meaning.**

Try this Prompt!
Dig out a failed first draft where you or your critique group felt the ending could have been better. Pick one of these six ending tips and rewrite your final stanza or two. Once you have the new ending, feel free to insert clues (especially if it's a twist ending) into earlier stanzas as well. Compare and contrast with your initial draft. Repeat this exercise with as many of the other techniques as you wish until you feel satisfied with the ending's resonance.

Pink-Cookie Lunch at the Circus: On Choosing Between Themes

My elder niece is five, a time I remember as both halcyon and horrible. I started school when I was five, I lost my first baby teeth and was given quarters under my pillow, and my sister was born. Quite a year!

When I consider writing a poem based on my kindergarten days, two experiences immediately assail me and both (in a different way) involve food and school. The first, a delicious burst of strawberry-cherry flavour that got stronger and better with each bite. The colour of the cookie was attractively bright as well. The surface was like shortbread: a bit cratered but soft, substantial, and crumbly when chewed. The cookie tucked neatly into a palm and although my taste buds would have gleefully eaten a sweet bouquet of them, we were granted one at a time. They arrived in our school lunch once or twice a month, but in kid time, it seemed an interminable wait of a blue moon until the next cookie showed up amidst the gross boxed milk I never drank (it tasted, to me, of grass), meat, vegetable (I spooned from side to side on the putty-coloured plastic tray), and thick slice of bread that smelled like the sponges we used to wipe the chalkboards but tasted yeasty and pleasant.

The only reason I recall these delectable desserts is due to the novelty of a brown-paper-bag lunch (when I brought lunch from home, which wasn't particularly often, it was carried in a pale-blue, cartoon-character lunchbox with matching mini thermos. How proud I was of that white-plastic-topped lid cup that I loved twisting in and out of place). Each of us kids was handed a paper bag as our bottoms bounced up and down from the hard, metal seats of bleachers, barely able to rip our attention away from the centre of the musty, circular tent as spangle-outfitted ladies loop-de-looped from swinging bars to catch each other and a guy with an old-timey top hat got an elephant to stand on a tiny chair.

Expecting little or nothing, I dipped my hand into the bag and emerged with a sandwich (likely bologna and government cheese) and, wonder of wonders, could it be? the coveted pink cookie! As per my usual, I half-heartedly munched at half the sandwich, chomped a bite or two of apple (I'm an earn-your-reward eater), and worked my way to the blissful, delicious pink treat as the lion tamer stepped into the ring. We all oohed and awed at the fat cat and his keeper. If I could have waved a fairy-godmother magic wand, I would have materialized a pink cookie (or 10) in school lunch Monday through Friday.

My second memory of that year involved chunky vomit. [Sorry, I never promised it would be pretty.]

From our assigned green seat, halfway back and to the left side of the bus, my seat mate, another girl in ponytails, barely had time to almost-whisper, "I don't feel good," amidst the ear-splitting cacophony-in-a-can that is a public-school bus in the afternoon, but she *did* have just enough time to turn her face to me and convulsively puke. It trickled down my hair. Onto the shoulders of my plaid dress. Splattered on my cotton white tights. It reeked, and it was not mine. Within seconds, my bus mates announced to the driver in shrieks that I stank. Well, no kidding. The driver, a bony, grey-haired Mennonite woman, responded by changing up the normal route. To take me and the puker home … dead last.

That's right—she did a U-turn to go out of her way to take home *the complainers* lest their tender nostrils be assailed by the noxious smell emanating from our seat and most of my person (the puker's corduroy pants were relatively unscathed).

My mom was worried that there had been an accident, as the bus was 45 minutes later than usual. The accident that met her when the squeaky doors peeled open was not the one she'd imagined. I was the final stop, and I remember my mom hurrying me with kind and tender, but efficient, steps inside our rental house, where I promptly started to weep. During the entirety of the bus ride, not one word of comfort or effort to clean me was made by the cranky kids (which I wouldn't now expect) or my driver (which I would; she should have known better, having grandkids my age).

Few things in life are as mortifying as wearing someone else's rotten stomach acids, friend or no. In a twist that would almost be too far-fetched for fiction, at a country fair eight years later, the same girl talked me into riding a ride called The Octopus, which spun our sugar-soaked stomachs both sideways and up-and-down; I nearly returned her favour, but I managed to return to sweet, grassy land with shaky limbs and pale face without parting ways with the candy apple and grease-soaked fries we'd scarfed down moments before our twist-fest.

What happens when two ideas—two compelling yet quite different ideas in tone and details—present themselves at once for poetic treatment?

- **Take some notes to keep the ideas warm while you decide which should come first.** Sometimes, I've started poems about one time or event only to find that the energy and pizzazz is in the other idea. No problem: if you take notes in a writing notebook when the two ideas hit, you'll easily be able to refer to what you've jotted—whether an image, line, or stanza—and add to or take from it in another draft.

- **Whether they took place in the same time period, as my above examples, or involve the same people or event, it's likely that these two ideas have something important yet unique to share with you and your audience. Ideally, I'd suggest you give both a shot. Sometimes, there might be a way to combine them into one poem (my favourite method) or into a series of poems. Other times, not so much.** In my above example, it could be that each idea would be a great individual poem in a thematic chapbook of poems about either kindergarten, being five, food, or early childhood memories.

- **Look for connection and common ground.** Even wildly disparate circumstances can be combined effectively at times. **If you're interested in trying to combine the ideas, ask yourself these guiding questions: Is there an image these two experiences or ideas share? Is there a catchphrase or idiom that these two ideas might have in common? What is the main theme of each idea?** For instance, will this be a poem about trust had and then lost? Will this be a poem about surprise—one surprise at the circus so delicious that even 35 years later I can close my eyes and taste that cookie—and one horrendous surprise? Are both ideas about food? Or peripherally about school? Could the alliterative, popping p's in "pink cookie" and "puke" be mined?

- **Embrace the friction.** While commonality is wonderful, opposites can sometimes mesh just as well. Paradox can work well when crafted with intention. Play up the friction. Juxtapose the tensions within a piece via opposing images, clashing tones, or seemingly dissimilar themes.

- **Do a free-write for each idea, even if it's weeks or months later. You'd be surprised just how easily you'll forget good ideas that flit through**

your head. Yeah, you think you'll remember, but you won't. Just humour me. Do your best to sort out the two strands now; even if one poem is more interesting or well-written than the other. Compare and contrast which version you like best. Which poem is most vibrant with specific detail and concrete imagery? Which poem recreates the experience while also having emotional resonance that sheds some new meaning on the experience or idea that you hadn't counted on? Save both drafts. I've had many drafts that seemed like duds that I put aside for another time—sometimes months or years later—only to resurrect and submit for publication when an aha! idea or phrase arrived.

Try this Prompt!
Choose a year in your past, any year.
What two events do you remember best from
that time? Jot notes for both. Write one poem
draft today. Save the other for later this week.
Compare and contrast drafts. Pick the poem
you think is strongest (outside opinions from
writing friends may be considered) and edit/
work on that one. Revisit the other draft
another day.

Poems of Longing, Loathing, and in-between Affection

When my sister last visited, we collaborated on a fun series of photos of her in historical dress, including a heavy satin ball gown, a 1930s white dress I found on-line, and several hats, one of which was wool. The day I photographed was my sister's next-to-last day in town, and our last chance before she packed up the girls and departed. It was the one day in an otherwise mild, dry August that was grey, overcast, thundery, and rainy. It was also 90 degrees and horribly humid.

Time after time, we ran into the wet grass at the first sight of drizzle letting up, hoping for some semblance of diffused sunlight—click-click-click—and then ducked back onto the porch.

Several of my favourite photos from the series have been published in *The Scene & Heard Journal.* Yet, one of the photos from the series that intrigues me the most is not one I'll ever submit because its technical proficiency is lacking. My nieces, who are generally encouraged to explore, were kept inside for as long as possible while we took as many photos as we could before the deluge commenced again. On the porch, the nieces easily wandered in and out of the house and underfoot, yelling across the yard, curious about what-in-the-world these strange grown-ups were doing.

I kept taking breaks, not wanting my good-sport sister to sweat through her gown or, worse, pass out after she was such a willing model and game for anything my zany photographer's brain imagined.

The instant we stepped foot back on the porch, Sylvie Ro buzzed underfoot, and I snapped a few photos of her with her green snack bowl in one hand, wrapping a silvery faux-silk scarf around her shoulders to make her feel included in the project. Turning around, I noticed Cora Vi without her glasses, bending over my sister who was reclining on a cool-stone ledge.

It's not a technically skilled photo. In haste, I've cropped my sister at an odd angle with her eyes half-closed, before my elder niece noticed me and moved away, self-conscious. But it's the devotion and curiosity with which Cora Vi stares down at her mother that intrigues—the way you look at someone you love whom you simultaneously feel comfortable enough to poke, prod, question, and explore as you tear them apart— the way we feel with intimates, particularly someone whose body once held our body while now, we are forever separate creatures.

In the photo, my niece is without her glasses that she wears all day. My sister is reclining in the shot; little sweat beads tumble from her grey gown's folds and she's just swatted away a swirl of them on her knees. The way my niece presides over my sister (who is usually quite tall, almost six feet) by standing on a deck chair and looking down at her, her face close to my sister's torso, inspecting with intense scrutiny, reminds me of the scene in *Young Frankenstein* where Gene Wilder's hair whips back in a frenzied wind and a stethoscope dangles from his ears.

Shortly after I snapped the photo, Cora Vi's tiny hands began to pat and prod my sister's shoulder and left arm, as if questioning whether different clothes made my sister a different person—tiny, exploratory jabs that caused my sister and me to chuckle and reminded us of the depth of that love-hate line.

Rarely is affection easy or uncomplicated. It's a natural human tendency to want to commemorate new love, long-term commitment, love-gone-wrong, and stages in-between. Not only do romantic and unrequited love make great subjects for poetry, but tenderness between friends and the platonic and intricate love we feel for family has also long inspired verse.

With such potential, why do some people roll their eyes at the thought of a love poem? **Sometimes, the idea of holding our loved ones up for inspection is overwhelming. We don't want to portray clichés, so we don't portray them or the feeling of love at all. There's also personal vulnerability in writing about private emotions.**

Plus, let's face it: there's a tendency to go saccharine and schmaltzy when penning new-love poems, before the shine wears off and an equal likelihood of bitterness or vindictive bile in the wake of soured friendships and romance. It's not easy to aim for middle ground, but it's often necessary when depicting amour or levels of fidelity.

When we write about bonds, we should keep in mind a few guidelines to ensure our poems are neither stock nor sentimental.

- **First, consider your audience.** If you're writing as a gift for a loved one and not planning on posting or publishing the work, then it might be appropriate to go full-throttle mushy. Why not? On the other hand, most of us *will* share our work with a larger audience, who likely won't connect to 100% idealism. If you're going to read your love poem at a spoken-word event or aim for publication in a chapbook or literary journal, try the next tips.

- **Focus on a particular moment or scene.** I never shared with you the thousands of hours my sister and I spent sharing a room growing up, but you get a sense of our continued bond via the one afternoon this year I described. So, too, should your poem highlight one specific setting yet demonstrate the connection between the speaker and another or between two characters.

- **Your addressee should be muddled, or at least a bit complex or conflicted.** No one likes to read poems from the perspective of someone who thinks they know it all or who flashes around their happiness. Ditto for poems about love interests who are perfection on two legs. In fact, Shakespeare's Sonnet 130 opens with acknowledging the lover's so-so, unconventional looks:

> My mistress' eyes are nothing like the sun;
> Coral is far more red than her lips' red;
> If snow be white, why then her breasts are dun;
> If hairs be wires, black wires grow on her head.

Not exactly flattering. He goes on to note she sometimes has bad breath in line eight! (Seriously; look it up.) Definitely not your typical, besotted boast to the beloved. Yet, by the poem's final four lines his open admiration and declaration of love for her seems all the more real for the fact that the woman *isn't* a hottie:

> I grant I never saw a goddess go;
> My mistress, when she walks, treads on the ground:
> And yet, by heaven, I think my love as rare
> As any she belied with false compare.

- **In praise poems, balance undying love with in-the-real traits, as Shakespeare does (although, keep in mind, he wrote most of his love sonnets on behalf of a patron, so it is likely someone else was love-struck with her eccentricities).**

- **Give your speaker some wily, idiosyncratic, humorous, or all-too-human qualities, too.** Aubades frequently feature coy pleas and flirtatious banter between parting lovers at dawn. One lover begs or teases their partner to stay longer. As a writer, aubades provide a chance to make a cleverly listed plea, to employ wickedly fun double-entendres, and/or pen melodic (sometimes alliterative) sound patterns to play up the flirtation. Richard Wilbur's "A Late Aubade" and Welsh singer-songwriter Jem's lush lyrics in "Stay Now" (https://genius.com/Jem-english-stay-now-lyrics) are excellent examples of this style of character development. Aubades give a sense of the loves' relationship and how one sweetheart has beguiled the other—and often, a hint foreshadowing why they'll tire of each other in the future.

- While the loved one is often addressed directly, whether in the title or body of the poem or both, **many great love (and hate) poems focus equally on the speaker's challenges and life issues or realizations.** While I often fly solo to visit my darling nieces and sister, I wrote the following poem when accompanying my parents on a grandchildren-seeing road trip to Missouri a few years ago.

"Ballad of the Turnpike"

For my nieces, Cora Vi and Sylvie Ro

I-76 merged with I-70 West
an hour ago
and all is tunnel,
green, green, green,
tunnel, green again.

It's rained for a week,
unseasonable and odd for June,
and now this canopy
like roadside broccoli stalks,
fresh florets
dropletted at the tippy-tops.

Each farm a picture postcard
from an earlier era
and yet, inexplicably, still here
to savour. Tunes unspool
in the car player. CDs I burned years
before your births—
Nick Drake, Jem, Fountains of Wayne,
The Flaming Lips—why has it been
so long? This humming along
this rattling ribbon of concrete?

When did I stop
singing like this every day?
When did I cease knowing
every new album's lyrics?

Every mile marker:
a rest stop, a gas up, a diner closer.
You and your sister
a day yet away,
keeping watch at the picture window.

I address my nieces and share my anticipation for seeing them soon. And yet, I ask some questions about the nature of spontaneous happiness, the fact that our cultural references slow and get dated with time as we age (and before we even realize it), and the pivotal role music plays in the lives of adolescents and young adults (band names are a wonderful way to evoke generation and/or time frame). Readers might also connect with how we might come to question ourselves and interpret our lives from a different perspective with a change of scenery. **Travel poems (whether by car, airplane, boat, or train) are a large subgenre of love and loss poems.**

Try this Prompt!
Either write a poem about a long-time platonic friend, noting the foibles that bond you, or write a love poem opening with your love's strange or quirky behaviour and then pivot to the passion in your last few lines, as Shakespeare does.

Scars and Stars and Tattoos: On Symbolism

It's less-than-an inch tall by less-than-an inch wide. It has no colour but a pattern, like a tooth print or tine print without the individual marks. Its shape is oblong-ish but not quite, and square but not entirely. It's on the left arm of my mother and the left arm of my father, although they are certainly not the only two who wear it.

What is it?

I recall touching it lightly with my fingers (as if it could bite me) as a preschool-age child when my mom cuddled me while reading a story. It looked like it would hurt, this vaccine mark, but my mom assured me it didn't hurt at all and it was to keep her from getting a horrible disease that some people got before a scientist had invented the medicine.

When will I get that mark? I wondered but didn't ask.

A few years later, in fourth grade, I'd contract chicken pox after a classmate's birthday slumber party. My mom would warn me and warn me and warn me not to scratch amidst the fever and itch ,and I didn't and I didn't and I didn't … until she left the room and I couldn't stand it one more moment. As I clawed my flesh to fleeting relief, I understood well the bliss my auntie's Boston Terrier experienced as his paws dug into the sweet red spot on his abdomen. My mom always walked back into the room, and I'd receive a stern scolding about scarring, but it was worth every last dig, even with the two permanent, eraser-sized scars I still carry.

For Baby Boomers, the polio vaccine scar is symbolic of an era where a reasonable fear was replaced with seemingly unending hope, a mark that has blended into their flesh and that they almost forget they carry until someone younger might ask when and if they notice. Today, my mom's vaccine mark is so faded that I wouldn't notice it at all when she wears short-sleeved or sleeveless shirts except that I remember it is there, right below her shoulder, in the muscled part that has carried children, grandchildren, and endless baskets of laundry in her strong arms.

My mom received the vaccine so young that she tells me she doesn't remember getting it—before school started, which, in those days, meant first grade. I forget about my chicken-pox marks for weeks at a time until I spot one at random in the mirror after a shower. In my late 20s, I met a man who had polio as a young boy, a few years before the vaccine was developed, and he told me tales of being encased in the iron lung for stretches at a time that felt like eternity. He still dealt with the medical effects as a 60-something-year-old man. The most jarring, intriguing poem I've read about this disease is Stanley Plumly's "Polio."

Consider the physicality of the body, whether in

the ravages of disease or in health, and speak to these images directly in your writing. Also consider how we mark the body through ritual or beauty practices such as piercing, pregnancy, and getting inked. Images with resonance provide a powerful way to explore themes in compressed language. Think of a friend's tattoos and stories the friend can tell based on the where, when, and what each ink represents. A few years ago, a student described to me (and then showed me) a fascinating Celtic-looking-design tattoo on his ankle that he, his parents, and his sister chose as a form of familial bonding, a forever-keepsake of their affection, right before he and his sister flew abroad to study in the States. One person, indeed one scar, can also become a symbol for a generation's medical improvement and an earlier generation's struggle. One symbol also stands for progress, for the Baby Boomers' youth, and the physical commonalities of fear, growth, decline, and emotional responses of all with the body gift. **Pair one symbol with another (or two) to develop a theme.**

Try this Prompt!
Make a list of your scars. If you
don't (yet) have any physical scars, list those
of someone you love or abhor. Then make
another list of cultural or personal symbols. You
might even list weather symbols. Pair images
from your scar list with images from your symbol
list and write a poem. The POV doesn't
have to be first-person, but it's certainly
welcome to be. Go!

The Jingle Jangle: On Diction Choices and Word Salads

"A POET IS, BEFORE ANYTHING ELSE, A PERSON WHO IS PASSIONATELY IN LOVE WITH LANGUAGE." —W.H. AUDEN

As an undergrad English major, I took a course called *Structure of the English Language.* Among many cool things I learned in the class—from how to break down sound patterns into glottal stops and fricatives to the reasons why there are regional dialects—I recall Professor L's discussion about how English is a polyglot. **English is the elastic band of languages.** It borrows words from across the globe and countless languages. It also becomes super creative once in a while and launches catchphrases that depict a place, time, or era that quickly become part of our lexicon, both verbally and on paper. *Tweet* and *bling*, anyone?

Most of the writers I know have been word-obsessed since their earliest memories. They have a natural sensitivity to how words are constructed and combined, the sounds they make, and both favourite and detested expressions. **Poets especially tend to be drawn to the verve and swing of each individual word chosen**

as well as how words interact in concert—the various shades of meaning between synonyms, the sound patterns that lead to musicality (such as soft m and n sounds), the staccato sounds (like k and t) that denote more frenzied, passionate emotions (and appear in most swear words), idioms from another era that sound slightly silly or amusing (*the bee's knees, far-out, good gravy*), catchphrases from advertising and sports, you name it. **With a language as amoeba-like and ever-growing, poets writing in English have an enormous palette of terms to sort through and choose.**

Gerard Manley Hopkins and e.e. cummings were innovators at pushing the boundaries of form and diction choices. Kaveh Akbar jumps to mind as a masterful innovator in the late 2010s. His poem, "River of Milk," demonstrates his playful and evocative use of figurative language as well as unique use of spacing within lines.

In fact, sometimes, the enormity of options can be overwhelming. Poets tend to work on drafts numerous times, workshopping and/or searching for "the best words in the best possible order," as Samuel Taylor Coleridge said. **While the intentions to communicate beautifully as well as effectively are important, we can overthink our options or become so obsessed with editing that our drafts get bogged or stalled in indecision.**

One of my favourite exercises when I teach poetry classes is something I call Word Salads. I choose eight or 10 unrelated words—they may be place names, other nouns, verbs, and every now and again an adjective or adverb. Students have to include at least three of the words in their drafts somewhere, along with any other words of their choosing. **It's amazing how limitations create poems that sing.** Poets begin to see connections in seemingly disparate words and write meaning where previously there was little or none.

Another fun exercise is to open a magazine or book of poetry and find two or three lines that are of interest from different pages. These lines will become separate lines of your new poem. Shaking up context and imposing parameters or guidelines can adjust the way our brains think about a stanza or line and free us from conventional, dictionary-bound definitions to a whimsical or intriguing new tone.

Try this Prompt!

Let's shake up content, context, and diction … into a Word Salad. Use at least three of these words in your poem today: Jordan (river or person's name), syncopation, murmur, wrapping paper, speedster, Gibraltar, sponge cake, rabbit's ear antennae, cloche, chimney flue.

A related alternative to this exercise which you can practice either alone or in a workshop setting and with endless permutations is to page through a dictionary and pick several words of your own choosing. You might also create your own word list and swap with a fellow poet—guaranteed to surprise and inspire. Then, without stopping, give yourself 20 minutes to make at least three of the chosen words into a poem. Go!

Travelling through Time: Shaking up Chronology

Sylvie Ro was wearing her ice-blue princess-gown pyja-mas as she climbed onto my sister's lap while the movie from the 1930s played. It was 20 minutes before bed-time, and Sylvie Ro was looking especially cute. As all people who feel joyful about their outfits, she was work-ing it with a jaunty expression and a hint of a swagger.

"Mama," she said sweetly.

"Yes, Sylvie."

Sylvie Ro wrapped an arm around her mother's back while looking at me in the armchair. My sister sat her knitting on the cushion beside her.

"I come from you belly one time," Sylvie Ro said and pointed.

"That's right," my sister trilled. "You were once right here in my belly."

"And Cora in you belly."

"Yep, Cora grew in my belly once, too."

"And ... " I could see the wheels in her head sparking like the glorious prize wheels at the country fairs when I was a kid. A quarter would buy a spin for a chance to win a fern, a giant bouffant-hair doll lamp with a sequin-laden parasol, or a huge stuffed dog with dangly ears. Even not winning a thing, it was worth it for the tick-tick-tick and anticipation as the pointer-pic flicked through each bead-tipped nail. This was going to be interesting, whatever pronouncement I was in for.

"And ... you in Nana's belly."

"That's right. I was once in Nana's belly," my sister affirmed.

Sylvie nodded. At two-and-a-half, so far so good. I smiled; my birthday-twin niece smiled back, patting her mother's back a little too hard.

"And Melmo ... "

"Yes, honey?" I asked, now thoroughly pulled from the black-and-white movie and anticipating her next pronouncement.

"Melmo, Pa T was in you belly."

My sister and I traded mirthful glances. "I'm afraid not, honey. Pa T is my daddy and your mama's daddy, so he was once in *his* mommy's belly. Your Great Grandma Faith's belly, a long, long time ago."

"Like you were once in Mama's belly." My sister explained patiently.

"That's right," I said, "Just like you were once in your mama's belly. Melmo has darling nieces, but no babies, which is cool, because being an auntie is amazing and her favourite thing. Pa T's mommy, though, had 11 babies. Can you imagine having 11 babies?" I asked, winking.

"Pa T *was* in you belly," she insisted, serious. "In *you* belly, Melmo," she repeated, and then climbed off her mother's lap and bounced away to her toy that she'd chucked onto the floor moments earlier.

Time. So often, we plan for our lives in neat rows—blocks on calendar pages to scroll or turn. This month, six months from now, next year. Infant, toddler, pre-schooler; elementary-, middle-, high-schooler; first job, college, graduate, first real job. Young, middle-aged, retiree. Spring, summer, autumn, winter.

In a sense, yes. In a larger sense, like Sylvie somehow comically tapped into: no. **Time is rolling in multiple directions at once, even though our brains construct things to feel like time is strictly chronological and individual.** The middle of my life's story-in-progress is the beginning of someone's story who was born this week and the end for someone who is near passing. Also, human nature—no matter what era—and to some extent the big human experiences (falling in love, loss and mourning, finding hope or forgiveness) often entail similar feelings, thoughts, and reactions no matter what year the calendar says.

On another level, too: **as writers, we have the option of flip-flopping through time**—travelling from a memory of a childhood fair, as I just did a few paragraphs ago—to something that happed three weeks ago, in the case of the Sylvie Ro anecdote, and then back to a time well before either of us had been born, as when I wrote a historical series of poems about the 1918 influenza outbreak in *This Passing Fever*. **As poets, we are not strapped in and forced to live 100% chronologically on the page. We can also make magical leaps through seasons, places, and settings. What freedom!**

Guess what: poetry can borrow and apply craft

ideas from its fiction and nonfiction cousins to great effect. Some cross-pollination of structures and time leaps between verse and prose can push exciting boundaries in your writing. Check out *How Fiction Works* by James Wood and *The Situation and the Story* by Vivian Gornick for more ideas.

All of our life's memories are at our disposal—rich and varied ground—to explore in any order we choose. **A poem about something that happened 25 years ago is just as valid as a poem about an event from last year and vice versa.** What's more—**even events and time periods we've never experienced first-hand are ours for the gleaning. If you need to (and why not?) read up on time periods that innately fascinate you, both online and in print editions, and jot some interesting facts to incorporate into new poems.**

Rather than staying locked within this year or even the year you were born, consider time as Sylvie Ro does and do some fanciful rearranging of facts and time travelling.

Try this Prompt!
Meet family, a friend, a co-worker,
or a neighbour for lunch and ask about
their earliest memories. Or their happiest
or saddest. Invite them to discuss their first
years as a student, their college years, or what
life was like as a newlywed or a young professional during another era. Then write a poem
loosely based on one of their life experiences.
Feel free to change details or time periods
or events as needed—even historical poems
don't have to be 100% chronological or fact-
based. Use these new-to-you remembered experiences as fresh settings and details to launch
your draft. If more than one poem idea or
draft arrives, feel free to take notes or even
to write more than one poem.

Alternate Prompt:
Research a historical time period and write a poem from the POV of a person whose life experiences were far different from your own. What would they want someone now to know? What did no one in their life understand about them at the time? Did they feel loved? Did they feel understood? Why or why not?

Buoyant Specks: Intermittency as Theme in Poetry

Hope can be an alluring double-edged sword and is the topic for many exquisite poems. Sometimes, hope works in our favour—most art works, public buildings, political campaigns, and organizations for social or personal change wouldn't have been formed without visionaries who consistently maintained and worked diligently for a better future even when the outcome wasn't promised or even obvious. But sometimes, such dogged belief in the invisible longshot causes stress, bitter disappointment, and what I like to call "the misery-go-round."

Psychologists have a term for the latter: *intermittent reinforcement.* It's what keeps children asking parents for dessert before dinner because they remember getting ice cream two or three times without eating their broccoli, despite hearing "no, eat your dinner first" the other 100 times. It's what keeps the dater checking text messages a dozen times a day to hear back from the would-be love who texted a total of twice in two months while ignoring the stable friendly messages about grabbing lunch from the better, more available love interest.

It's what keeps the employee at the dead-end job where advancement is slim-to-none because every few weeks, a higher-up dangles the carrot of restructuring and a new appointment she'd be "perfect" for in the "near future" if she can "just hold on a bit longer and finish this project." Sound familiar?

What is it about the long shot that makes it so dazzlingly appealing? Perhaps it's scarcity. Or the fear of missing out on an opportunity the second one decides to throw in the towel and then watching someone who did next-to-nothing receive our rewards.

More often, though, it's plain imagination. Yep, fantasy can be a real head trip. Again, something that keeps us sane and satisfied and striving for better in the midst of troubles and trials delivers the old one-two punch. When a situation or person is rare and just-distant enough to be a possibility without a reality, we can project whatever feelings, thoughts, or dreams we want onto them without the killjoy of ordinary-life restrictions.

It's not all bad news: when we wonder how much a company, a person, or a group has invested in us, for a while this instability works to motivate our actions and elevate our moods. I'll be honest—I love few things more than a project and a goal. As an introverted INFJ (check out personality types at the Myers-Briggs type-indicator site: www.myersbriggs.org) and a glass-half-full dreamer, I can reside in Anticipation Station for ridiculous stretches. I enjoy organizing large, long-term ideas into bite-size, possible portions (like this book, for instance). If it's a with-enough-steady-work-you-can-accomplish-anything person you're needing, look no further and please step out of the way—I'll be first in line and complete the task, probably before deadline (preferably alone, with few interruptions, and at my own rocket-to-the-goal pacing). The traits that serve me beautifully in my writing life and friendships don't tend to pan out as well for money-making ventures nor for romantic security. I've hung onto expectation way past the point when most logical people would forfeit prospects and save themselves the pervasive disappointment. But not for forever. We all have limits. We all can stand knocking at a closed door for just so long until—no, we don't give up, we just proceed to the next door.

Hope and our reactions to it or lack of it make a meaningful theme for verse because:

- **it mirrors the intermittent reinforcement in so many parts of life—from finances to weight-loss or weight-gain to romance to reward for a job well done.** Yes, sometimes, we get the responses and reactions and spoils we want ... but not always when we yearn for them and not even often. **As compressed language, poetry has a unique way of emphasizing the juxtaposition between expectation and reality, especially in final stanzas and/or final lines.**

- **it's part of the human condition to want what we think is better than what we have now and to be confused about how to obtain our longings.** No matter what our backgrounds, ages, races, genders, or education-levels, we all experience hope and its close kin, loss—two sides of the same sword, both inspiring topics for art.

- **much like journaling, poetry can help us process experiences that were painful or joyful or a confusing mixture of both.**

Other poets address this theme head-on, as in this poem by Emily Dickinson (who I will forever call Ms Emily):

"'Hope' is the thing with feathers"

"Hope" is the thing with feathers -
That perches in the soul -
And sings the tune without the words -
And never stops - at all -

And sweetest - in the Gale - is heard -
And sore must be the storm -
That could abash the little Bird
That kept so many warm -

I've heard it in the chillest land -
And on the strangest Sea -
Yet - never - in Extremity,
It asked a crumb - of me.

Those feathers, symbols of lightness and fleeting feelings! Those emphatic, emotional dashes and exclamation marks! The storm imagery and her emphatic capitals where no capitals should be (Gale, Bird, Sea, Extremity)! Ms Emily's tone frantically broadcasts flights of fancy that were rare in their sweetness (many of her other poems focus on mortality and disappointment, which makes this one all the sweeter). Incidentally, deep Ms Emily and one of my other favourite old-school literary rock stars, Jane Austen, share my December birth month.

Another approach to this topic is with *saudade*—a Portuguese term for bittersweet longing—in this case, for the past and a long-ago love, by Laurence Hope:

"Kashmiri Song"

Pale hands I loved beside the Shalimar,
    Where are you now? Who lies beneath your spell?
Whom do you lead on Rapture's roadway, far,
    Before you agonise them in farewell?

Oh, pale dispensers of my Joys and Pains,
    Holding the doors of Heaven and of Hell,
How the hot blood rushed wildly through the veins,
    Beneath your touch, until you waved farewell.

Pale hands, pink tipped, like Lotus buds that float
    On those cool waters where we used to dwell,
I would have rather felt you round my throat,
    Crushing out life, than waving me farewell!

Note the rhythmic end rhymes along with the imagery (pale hands, hot blood through veins, hands "pink-tipped, like lotus buds that float," the throat, a wave farewell). The repetition of the "pale hands" also underscores the obsessiveness of memory and yearning.

Try this Prompt!
Write a quick list of three or four times when you've experienced intermittent reinforcement, whether the recipient or the giver of such lagging hope. Pick one instance and write about the experience for 15 minutes. Why does the speaker hold on for so long? Is it a good waiting period? An agonizing one? Or both? At the end of 15 minutes, take your notes and pen a poem, including symbolic images to demonstrate the highs, lows, or mixtures of emotions, as with Ms Emily's feathers and Gales and Laurence Hope's hands and lotus.

Penmanship Party: Mining the Past for Poetry

I'm a sucker for a handwritten notecard.

The distinctive loops or lines, flourishes or fierce angles of each letter add that little something extra to a plain old message. Not to mention the different kinds and hues of ink. Like most people in the 21ˢᵗcentury, I spend my life typing and staring at screens most of the day. While I'm grateful for the technology that has allowed me to expand my teaching and writing careers and to connect easily with my readers and editors, I savour the retro reach of a tactile, old-school paragraph written in cursive back when I learnt it in third grade.

It's a fluid yet highly personal way to write. There's something connective about the press of our fingers on the pen and across the cardstock—a feather-dusting of DNA and deep thinking that go hand-in-hand. On-screen communication, while easier in some ways, is flat and one-size-fits-all by comparison.

Since 2000, many schools in the US have stopped teaching penmanship and handwriting altogether, much to my disappointment (not that I was consulted). Students still learned to print, of course, but a few years ago, my high schoolers started telling me they couldn't read anything I wrote on the board in cursive.

The New York Daily News and *Business Insider* both ran articles on this topic in 2017. Fifteen states have reinstated cursive proficiency for public schools. While that's not a majority of schools changing their cursive-teaching policy, it's enough to suggest there's a rising tide of support for bringing back this crucial learning tool and art form.

Now, admittedly, my handwriting is not what I'd call Palmer Method by any stretch. My lowercase g's look almost like f's or undotted j's, especially in the middle of words. When ideas get flowing, I have a tendency to write uphill while I'm talking through various points. Still, I much prefer writing in cursive in notebooks and on other surfaces—not only is it faster mechanically and mentally, but it's also vastly satisfying compared to my plodding printing.

Yet I didn't want my high-schoolers to be clueless, and there was more-than-enough literary analysis, vocabulary, and paragraph structure to be taught to preclude cursive on the lesson list, so I switched and started outlining and jotting notes entirely in print. I still don't love it, but I've learned to live with it and meet the students where they are. Anything to facilitate student learning.

On the other hand, imagine my glee when visiting my sister this summer and she took me with her to the school-supply store to peruse textbooks for my kindergarten niece. When she read from the book-list that my elder niece's private school has put handwriting back on the curriculum and that she'll be learning the art this year, I almost requested a penmanship party and high-fived my sister right there in Aisle 27. I write my nieces notecards (splashed with unicorns, kittens, puppies, or other niece-friendly designs) on Fridays and snail-mail them each Saturday, so I immediately envisioned my nieces ripping shards into the pastel envelopes and reading my messages aloud for themselves soon. I also can't wait to see if their script will be precise, highly vertical, and easy-to-read like their Nana's, scribblier and slant like mine, or somewhere in-between.

In addition, there's the continuity of it—the kind of writing my ancestors did with quill and ink well, the kind of writing I learned in the mid-1980s with a stubby, yellow, number-two pencil, my nieces taking up the strand of it far beyond my generation. **It's a fulfilling feeling to be a spot along the way, with connections trailing behind and ribbons unspooling in front of me.**

Why write about the past?

- **Like it or not, events from the past inform the present. As William Faulkner so famously said: "The past is never dead. It's not even past."**

- **Catharsis.** We often suppress painful or confusing events from our past, yet they resurface in dreams or at unexpected moments. Why not let that past resurface on the plain page where it can be sculpted into art?

- **The past is often filled with images and symbols that contain deeply ingrained cultural and**

personal meanings. Perhaps when you see ice skates, you flash back to your first crush, meeting your neighbours on the pond once the ice finally froze over, or your first broken leg. Rich territory for poetry.

- **No matter how unremarkable you think your experiences have been** (and I'm betting they haven't been, as we often forget through time the details that made our experiences unique), **there's no one else who can present your memories the same way you can.** Like cursive writing on a page, **you have a distinct voice, tone, and diction style that no one else can duplicate.**

- **Writing about the past can be tremendous fun.** Not all writing about the past is depressing or morbid. Sometimes, we write about the past as a form of celebration or to share amusing memories.

One of my favourite Flannery O'Connor quotes applies here: **"Anybody who has survived his childhood has enough information about life to last him the rest of his days."** No matter your age, you have a storehouse of possible topics to mine.

Get to it. You can bet I'll be writing many of mine both on the screen as poems and in cursive on notecards with hearts and ponies.

Try this Prompt!

Create a gigantic list of memories. It doesn't matter what years, eras, or locations you explore. They don't have to be in any kind of chronological order; in fact, feel free to jump back and forth in time and place. You may choose to jot the names of a few people you were with and/or snippets of dialogue or images that stick out in your mind, although give each memory just a few lines maximum. Number each note as you add to it. During your next free-write, choose one of the memories and write a short poem centring not only on your note but on anything else that arises in your memory as you draft.

Keep your list handy (if you write it in a writer's notebook, skip a few pages after you think your list is over—like rabbits from a magician's hat, one memory tends to lead to 100); add to your topic list as inspiration continues to strike.

Section II
It's Time I
Made it To the
Top: Editing,
Workshopping,
and Publication

The Synaptic Surge of a Writing Challenge: Five Tips for Initiating and Enjoying a Work Swap

Today is Halloween, but an even more exciting event for me personally. It is the victory-dance day in a poetry-swapping challenge a dear friend, C, and I started 31 days ago. We sent our final poems to each other's inboxes this morning, winging their way from our minds to our desks and portable devices, from three states away and straight to a dedicated reader and fellow author.

The feeling of accomplishment is real, even if the poems are sometimes limping along in first-draft stages. **We now have 31 fresh drafts to sculpt, edit, and arrange any time we'd like to do a free-write.** [*Insert confetti and balloons here.* In fact, that's exactly what I wrote in the subject heading of today's emailed draft.]

If you've never participated in a poetry-draft swap before, I highly encourage it. **Ideally, choose someone you've known for a while and know you can rely on to submit work each day. The practice of daily submissions can inject your writing with a new energy and gusto.**

Choose someone of your skill level but who might also have talents or poetic interests that you don't have to broaden your own range. My friend is also a high-school teacher. He writes primarily rhymed formal verse (his sonnets are exquisite!), while I am primarily a free-verse and prose-poem writer. We share a love for the nuances and silvery swing of language. We share just enough in common—often writing about nature, family, or life observations—that we are cheerleaders for each other and can offer specific, helpful advice on ways to make each draft just that much better at a future date. Yet we are different enough—he is a Baby Boomer Southern gentleman, father, and grandfather, while I am a Gen X, East Coast auntie—that we bring outlooks and strengths to the table that are useful and perhaps not something the other poet would have thought of on their own.

Your writing can also be enriched by setting up an informal swap with a fellow writer. Here are five tips for initiating and carrying through the kind of poetry swap that will not only keep you writing but make the journey inspiring each day.

- **I highly recommend asking at least three or four weeks ahead of a swap's start date**, in case the other person has a particularly busy week or month now but may still be interested in choosing another time to swap work with you. Sometimes, C initiates a swap and sometimes, I do. We email each other several weeks or months ahead of time to choose a mutually beneficial time, which is the only way either of us could plan to have enough energy left at the end of the day to crank out a draft in our busy schedules. As educators, September and May are paperwork minefields we have always avoided.

- **Agree to a certain amount of days ahead of time. Don't be ambiguous, thinking it will all fall into place.** Look, I'm loosey-goosey in a lot of ways, letting circumstances array themselves as they will or need to. However, when it comes to my writing, I don't play. **When you agree to trade work with someone, know exactly how long it will last and commit to it as you would to being on time to your day job or being at your kid's soccer practice to see them play.** Before you get started, you must know when your goal ends so that you can know just how many poems you'll be writing (and reading from your friend) this month and how much feedback your partner anticipates. **Communicate clearly your own feedback goals with your swap partner.** Would you like suggestions for titles, phrasing, or other parts of your poem that you'll inquire about when you send the poem, or would you rather just share the poem and let your partner comment on whatever they feel is needed?

- **When you ask a writer if they'd like to swap, make it a reasonable amount of time.** Daily for a month for the first swap is quite a lot to ask of anyone. You can agree to once-a-day for a week or to swap one or two poems a month for, say, three months on the first day of the month to get going. Years ago, when we first started to swap, C and I agreed to trade three poems once a month for the first few swaps to ease into the process. Once we knew that we worked well together, then one of us (it's been 11 years, so I can't remember whom!) asked the other about a possible whole-month swap.

- **Once you've successfully set up a swap, send some feedback about the day's poem.** Don't overwhelm with many paragraphs, but a few sentences of hello and to describe your experience with the poem or a line or two or a title you are wondering about are well within your bounds and will keep the swap lively. Always remember that this person is taking time out of their regularly scheduled day to read your work. Value that rare dedication and the time away from their own work that this support takes.

- **Offer encouragement back. Once you receive and read the other person's poem, give it a second and third read.** Pick one or two complimentable areas (such as an eloquent phrase or line or stanza, specific diction choices that make the poem memorable) and offer that to your fellow poet. Also offer an appropriate suggestion or two. **That said, it's important not to pick the poem apart—these are just drafts, after all—**while doing a close read that respects the fellow poet's work. Areas of suggestion might include: the title, an ambiguous pronoun, a noun or verb that could be more specific, details that might be added or omitted, the poem's format (perhaps the poem is already 14 lines and, with some rhyming and syntax changes, could make a meaningful sonnet), or questions you have about the poem's narrative.

Any month is a perfect month for a poetry challenge. Novelists have NaNoWriMo (National Novel Writing Month) during which participants agree to write daily for 30 days each November. Well, guess what we have: NaPoWriMo. April may be "the cruellest month," but it's celebration time for poets. **Every April (National Poetry Writing Month), poets across the US and abroad take part in slam-poetry events and readings, newsletters, writing workshops and seminars, and daily informal poetry swaps** just as the grass is turning green and flowers are teasing us with their budding potential. Consider marking it on your next calendar and lining up a few poetry readers and writers to take part in some daily verse fun.

Try this Prompt!
Take an honest look at your schedule
for the next six months. If you were
to set up a poem challenge, when might be the
ideal date for starting? (Keep in mind that many
months have national or personal holidays that
require extra planning and time that might impact your
writing availability. If you work a job that requires time-
consuming obligations at certain times of year, such as
the wedding and floral industries, food industries, or
academia, plan accordingly.)
Write about your ideal swap for 15 minutes.
How many poems would you swap? Would it be
a once-a-week swap, a once-a-month swap, or a
daily swap? How long would the challenge last?
What kinds of comments/compliments might you
offer about the other poet's writing? What would
you like to hear about your writing, and how do you
think a swap will help your writing to grow?
After a few minutes of free-writing your ideal writing challenge, **think of three possible candidates**
for a swap. Contact the first person on your list
to see about setting up a mutually ben-
eficial writing challenge in real-time.

The Art of Offering Feedback: Real-World Tips for Helpful Poetry Critiques

Writing can be a solitary craft, yet there are many ideal ways to connect with other poets and grow our writing skills in the process. Workshops. Classes. Beta readers. Poem-swap buddies.

One of the best ways to become better poets is regularly to share our work with other writers working towards the same goals of clarity, beauty, and fluidity. Offering suggestions on others' work, we writers learn more about how our own poems work, how current and future poems might be improved, and our own poetic and editorial preferences in theme, tone, style, and more.

What makes a good critique?

- **Honesty and clarity.** Don't compliment parts just to have something to say—instead, reach for an excerpt you truly admire and then briefly explain why you admire it.

- **Specify, specify, specify.** Choose one or two intriguing, fresh insights that the poem provides and articulate why those word choices, lines, or stanzas resonate with you as a reader. The more specific you can be the better. An entirely negative critique, a gushingly positive statement, or a critique that is vague ("Great job!" Or, conversely, "This is stupid.") won't give the author enough to begin seeing their poem as the reader does. Mention specific words, lines, or stanzas so that the author can reference the parts you find vague, the alliteration you liked, and the two lines in stanza four that were confusing.

- **Encouragement.** Even if this style of poem isn't what you prefer (perhaps it's a sestina but you write free-verse) or about a topic you've read a million times, point out what the poet is doing well. There will be something in every draft—even if it's a beautiful title, a word choice, or a cool setting. Writers frequently realize drafts need improvement, so when making suggestions, offer them with a professional tone. **Respect that this is another writer's work and that you are providing a supportive viewpoint which they are under no obligation to follow or to change their work.**

Tips for offering helpful feedback:

- **Compliment a phrase or word choice(s) that resonates with you. Say what you like about this diction choice. Specific feedback is most helpful.**

- Consider theme. Does the poem explore a certain leitmotif? Is all of the language and syntax appropriate for the theme? You might want to begin your comments with: To me, this poem is about_____, which is an excellent way to show your fellow writer how you are interpreting what they've written, whether the way the poet has intended or not. This feedback will also give the writer an opportunity to adjust their draft accordingly.

- Note the stanza or lines you like best. Explain. Also, consider where stanzas and lines end. If you notice any patterns with line-breaks or where lines begin (such as anaphora or the repetition of a phrase at the beginning of several lines in a row for artistic resonance and emphasis), note them. You might also offer suggestions for where a line or stanza might begin or end with more impact and why.

- Comment on the title. Does the title invite readers into the poem without giving away too much of the poem's plot? If not, look within the poem's body for another title or offer suggestions for other titles that might match the poem's theme better.

- Does the poem employ a strong, end-line rhyme scheme in the first few lines and not follow that pattern later in the poem? If so, gently point it out.

- Poems often make allusions to places, literary figures/celebrities/artists, cultural icons, and even other poems. Note any you spot and explain if they are fitting or not.

- Remember: poems share many literary similarities with their prose cousins: What is the poem's setting? Does the poem have characters, including a protagonist and antagonist and/or supporting characters? What is the main conflict within the poem? List them, citing specific line references for your notes.

- Jot any questions you might have about the poem. Are there omitted words or phrases (which often happens in the heat of drafting)? Does the poem begin with one idea and then veer off into another without finishing the first idea? Do you wonder what happens to the protagonist in a certain line? Are there pronoun confusions or ambiguous references? Gently note them.

Keep in Mind:

- These are drafts so spelling errors, repetitions, inconsistencies, and such are likely. You can point out one if you want, but don't nit-pick on small errors that the author will catch on their own later. Think big picture: theme, character, setting, dialogue, conflict, and other literary devices or parts of a possible story arc.

- Many workshops use the "compliment sandwich method" of feedback: offer one compliment, ask a question or point out a confusing passage, finish with another compliment. You don't have to follow this format, but it's worth considering.

- Remember that it takes a lot of courage to share one's writing. Follow the Golden Rule, and don't dish out vague or purposely hurtful feedback you wouldn't want to receive about your own writing.

Try this Prompt!
Make a poetry-swap friend at a workshop, class, or online. Agree to share work once a month. When you send your work, note one area that you're wondering about and one area that you feel went well with the poem. Consider using the above guidelines as you offer feedback, suggestions, and support to your fellow artist.

If the Shoe Fits: Meditations on Poetic Form

If you wanted to describe the shade of them, I'd say: lavender mixed with wood-stove ash. The official hue on the receipt was something chic-sounding with the whiff of the exotic, like Loden.

My latest pair of shoes is perfect for this in-between time of year—when August is giving way to signs of September—spider webs lacing lawn furniture, sunflowers with their burnished, bright faces—and yet, the snap of cold isn't here yet. A time more substantial than sandals and less carefree, foretelling the early autumn leaf-fall and paperwork ahead of me.

The sole is a springy sneaker rubber, almost entirely hidden by the "upper," in a shade meant to camouflage itself with its unassuming beigeness. *I'm barely here; just quietly doing my job for your comfort,* they convey. It's some kind of scientifically tested sole much-squawked about online that is engineered lighter than ever and yet more comfortable. I tell you what's comfortable: the built-in cushiony inserts in these babies. When I flopped them onto the discount chain's hard, shiny floor and slipped my barking dogs into them the first time, I could not contain the "ahhh … " that escaped my lips. That, alone, earned them a direct trip into my basket.

The upper itself, with its boat-shoe shape and soft almost-suede finish, resembles what I've seen in glossy magazines called "driving moccasins," although I am several tax brackets below the kind of person who drops that term into my daily talk.

I was decidedly not in the market for shoes. I should say, *more* shoes. Truthfully, I need more shoes like I need more pens: my purse, my closet, and my person overflows with them. And yet … I spotted them in Aisle 7.5. They were discounted to less than a third of their original price. They were a brand I recognized and already own. Okay, they wouldn't win any sexiness prize, but as a friend of mine several years my senior once quipped, "I'm getting too wise to suffer through painful shoes or jerks anymore, no matter how cute."

How would the shoes fit into my daily life? Would they remain parked at the back of my closet, after rubbing my Achilles heel blistery one-too-many times? I envisioned them with a dark pair of jeans and sweater while the leaves turn sepia and scarlet and I haul a heavy bag of texts across campus, I envisioned them with a long skirt and a cardy on the weekends while writing or with family, I envisioned throwing them on almost any day with my hair pulled into a ponytail to make the trek to get the mail. Yes, yes, yes. They fit perfectly. Mine.

How do we know the perfect form our verse should take? Some poets believe the poem is in control of choosing a form for itself, others feel strongly that the poem itself chooses its form. Either way, **as with shoe-shopping, there are a myriad of styles**, line lengths, and stanza formations a poem can take. **While no one-size-fits-all approach exists, here is a checklist of questions to consider for discerning the best fit for your poem.**

- **Are there any discernible patterns?** For instance, is there a kind of refrain or a repetition? If so, that might point the way to a formal structure, such as terza rima or a villanelle, where rhymes and repetitions are key. One of the most famous villanelles that would be ideal to study for patterns and rhyme scheme is Dylan Thomas' "Do Not Go Gentle into That Good Night." For sonnets, you can't go wrong with any of Shakespeare's or Petrarch's. No worries if neither of these formalist forms interest you: there are plenty of other types. I recall being introduced to ghazals, a Persian list form, in grad school and finding them fascinating (and a bit easier to manage than sestinas). To learn more, look up Ellen Doré Watson's "Ghazal." Want another whirl, try a pantoum, a Malayan form made up of refrains. A wonderful and playful example of the pantoum form is "Parent's Pantoum" by Carolyn Kizer. Marilyn Hacker's "Iva's Pantoum" is also evocative and instructive. Don't ask me why so many pantoums have the title "pantoum" in them!

- **Does your poem include a rhyme pattern, es-**

pecially at the ends of lines? If so, once again, you might have a formal structure that would best serve the work, such as a sestina. For a sestina to study and inspire, try two of Elizabeth Bishop's poems: "A Miracle for Breakfast" and "Sestina."

- **Does your poem focus on one quick moment in time and then veer to another in a flash?** In that case, a Tanka or haiku might be of interest, especially if you have focused nature imagery and/or could omit lines that are unimportant to the crux of the poem.

- **Does your poem revolve around one particular event or moment in time?** Does it shine a light on a happening with a zoom lens? In that case, a poem with just one stanza, called a stichic, could work well.

- **Does your poem include several parts? Does each part relate to the other parts and yet also move forward in time or topic in some way?** In that case, you might have a longer poem, where each stanza (or every few stanzas) becomes a numbered or lettered section. You might also consider subtitling each section with a word or phrase related to the theme, something to denote how each part is connected to the work as a whole.

- **Does your poem have long lines that are almost (if not entirely) wrap-around text, in the style of Walt Whitman, where imagery or even** listing of symbols occurs? Does your poem explore a persona or a character in a quirky or strange situation, such as Russell Edson's "Ape?" A prose poem might be worth exploring.

- **Does your poem have line breaks that you created to shed light on a particular word or phrase? Or does your poem have line or stanza breaks that you inherently felt and made as you composed?** In this case, free-verse might be your best bet. Feel free to move those line or stanza breaks for maximum resonance and emphasis while editing.

Try this Prompt!
Use this checklist on a draft you have shelved or that has stalled previously. Choose one of the sets of questions and change the format of your poem, based on the suggestions above. Look up at least two examples of the form you've chosen, to serve as inspiration for the editing process.

The Plandid and Other Splendid Editing Options

"THE BEAUTIFUL PART OF WRITING IS THAT YOU DON'T HAVE TO GET IT RIGHT THE FIRST TIME, UNLIKE, SAY, A BRAIN SURGEON." —ROBERT CORMIER

Yesterday, I read an article about iconic visual artist Cindy Sherman who has made a career out of taking evocative self-portraits in various guises. I learned a new term thanks to her interviewer: the "plandid." In our selfie-obsessed world, meet the "planned candid." For the record, it was only the interviewer who used this term; Sherman made it clear she doesn't consider her work plandids or selfies.

For plandids, gathering props and outfits, brainstorming and nabbing the perfect setting, and even taking notes or drawing sketches is fair game to make the final shot(s) appear effortless. **It's a form of editing before crafting the work.**

Subterfuge much? Actually, not.

As a just-starting-out, unpublished author, I never thought much about the art of editing. In fact, I didn't consider editing an art at all. Nor did I believe in the need to plan before beginning a draft. Something within me curled up and snarled like a dog on a leash at the thought of cutting into anything I'd written. It would spoil the spontaneity! It would mar my creation to pick and choose and leave little pockmarks on my lovely lines!

Then, I had two experiences that opened my mind. One with an editor who made suggestions to a submitted piece and offered publication *if* I'd be willing to follow some of suggestions. I typed a new draft using about 75% of his suggestions and printed it. Comparing the hard copies, I realized that his ideas elevated my piece. By this point, I'd had two or three short stories and some poems published and participated in a reading or two, but never before had I noticed the give-and-take between editor and writer—or that **a talented editor can sculpt a piece, maintaining the author's original intention, tone, and theme while making it, yes!, even clearer and more vivid.** My editor was happy, I was happy; publication ensued.

A few years later, I started graduate school for a Masters in Fine Arts where there was a heavy emphasis on workshopping. Each month, I received feedback from four or five other writers alongside the suggestions of my professor, a highly published creative writer. **I learnt how to listen to options with an open heart, sift through what might work, experiment with my drafts, and let go of suggestions or comments that just didn't work for my intentions for the piece. Best of all, the process taught me a lot of tricks for editing my next poems. Suggestions I'll happily share.**

You might find your own poems need other kinds

of feedback—which is certainly valid—as this is certainly not a comprehensive or one-size-fits-all list. On the other hand, **it can be enormously helpful to keep some guidelines in your poetic toolbox as you write and revise, especially if you would like to publish.** To gain perspective to assess your writing's strengths and weaknesses can take a while, but it's both an insightful and exciting journey.

Use these tips as guidelines to get you started on self-editing, and remember that informal writing swaps, workshops with fellow authors (if you don't know of one your community, join one online or start one), and professional freelance editors (often available at reasonable rates for small chapbooks or batches of poems) are other motivating resources for sharpening your skills and sculpting your poems.

- **What is your first line or stanza? Is it on-topic? Does it hook your reader, or is it the equivalent of a vocal warm up? Is there a line or stanza later in the poem that would better serve the poem? Remember: each part of a draft is moveable.** Try another opening line—whether an excerpt from later in the poem or entirely new.

- **Catch and clear the clutter. Are there prepositional phrases that lengthen your lines but don't serve much purpose to the poem's theme?** Compress or omit them. Are there double or triple adjectives in a row? Narrow it down to one. Or, even better: **use a dynamic noun and omit the adjective.** Instead of fancy, big, expensive dress: gown.

- **Where do you have repetitions? Are they on purpose or accidental?** In poetry, all repetitions must serve a purpose in the narrative. If they are anaphora or a refrain, they get to stay, but if they are the accidental use of the same word on two different lines, change one. Do you "Find and Replace" for redundant repetitions; I'll be honest: I had over 70 uses of "great" and 60 uses of "good" when I first began editing this book.

- **What sound patterns do you use?** Even if your poems don't rhyme, verse is a musical medium. Consider that as you make diction choices. Are there passages where you can add alliteration? What about approximate rhymes mid-line? How about a synonym with a hard d, p, or t sound to connote tension and anger rather than a word with soft m or n sounds?

- **Study where you break new lines and stanzas. Do you (sometimes) end mid-punctuation or always end-stop lines. What effect does that have on your reader's experience of the poem?** Read your work out loud to see where the rhythm could be better-paced. Did you leave any blank space at all? **Remember—much like in the visual arts, your poem lives as a shape and style on the page; some empty space gives the work room to breathe and room for the readers to process your meaning.** Aim to end and begin lines on dynamic words rather than prepositions and articles.

- **What figurative language is included in your poem?** While it's not a requirement to include imagery or similes and metaphors, many poems do employ them because such figurative language expresses much concisely. Are the images you've chosen in service of the poem's theme and tone?

- **Do you mix metaphors anywhere in the poem?** For instance, if your poem is about summer camp and you compare a see-saw to a crock-pot/slow-cooker, it's likely you've mixed metaphors, as these two objects have almost nothing in common. Make sure your metaphors match your theme. If you have several uses of figurative language, increase the symbolism: make all of them about similar ideas. For instance: if I wrote a poem about Lake Gitche Gumee and included metaphors about tubing, water droplets, and swimsuits, there would be a cohesion to the poem that would be lessened if I had one metaphor about tubing and the others focused on tennis and basketball. In poetry, you should **seek smooth, seamless cohesion, like a laser beam's focus.**

- **If your poem includes a character or two, did you include monologue or dialogue? This is certainly not required, but some character-based poems include snippets of a character's conversations or inner thoughts. Does the dialogue serve the theme and plot of the poem?** Does it develop the character and match other things the character has said or done in related poems? **As in fiction, dialogue should be spare yet develop characterization or conflict.** There's not room in a poem for "Have a nice day" or "Good to see you," which is filler language. try: "You always say that."

- **How does your poem end? Does the concluding idea resonate and invite the reader to another read of the work? If so—excellent; you have a keeper. Does your poem continue past the most resonant ending? Might there be lines you can omit from the end and use elsewhere in the poem or not at all?** In initial drafts, it's common to have a few extra lines at the end while figuring out how the poem works—play with those lines to see if they might be better elsewhere or if your current ending sheds light on the poem's purpose. **Remember that a poem doesn't have to tidily sum up the main idea—in fact, abrupt or repetitious conclusions are boring. Many of the best poems make a suggestion through an image or a metaphor that invites reader interpretation long after reading the work.**

- **Once you've gone through the body of your poem, consider your title.** It's the way you'll greet your readers, so it should be specific but not too telling; thematic but not too mechanical. James Wright gets my vote for one of the best, most descriptive titles: "Lying in a Hammock at William Duffy's Farm in Pine Island, Minnesota." Don't you want to know what happens next?

He includes place/setting in such an inviting way without cluing us into much about the speaker, thus inviting us to find out for ourselves. Titles don't need to be long, however: "The Raven," is succinct and to-the-point, yet also specific. Connotations of a dark bird instantly spring to mind, which wouldn't have been nearly as effective if Poe had titled the poem: "The Bird." Long or short, **aim for specificity when you can.**

- **Ask yourself: What is the theme of my poem? Encapsulate it in a sentence.** Now read through the entire poem, making sure every phrase, line, and stanza builds on that theme. Any pieces that are extra information must go. **If you don't know what your poem is about in a few words, go back and do a free-write to excavate more material.** You might glean enough material for a few more poems or find the perfect snippet to develop the current poem. Either way: win-win. **Other questions to ask as you edit: So what? and What is at stake in the poem? What is at stake for the reader?**

Try this Prompt!
Take your draft through the 10
tips above, making notes on which areas are
working well and which areas you might move,
rewrite, or omit to strengthen the work.
Make a few edits, print before-and-after copies of
both drafts, and compare. Which draft serves
the poem's topic best? **Editing is about making
great even better.** Feel free to repeat these
steps a few times—adding, omitting, and
moving—until you have struck the right
balance for your poem.

Wild Cards: Eight Tips for Choosing Poems for Submission

"LIFE IS SHORT, ART LONG, OPPORTUNITY FLEETING, EXPERIENCE TREACHEROUS, JUDGMENT DIFFICULT." —HIPPOCRATES

"Watch me colour!" my elder niece calls as I leave the table to fill my water glass.

"Watch me!" my younger niece parrots. "Watch me!"

"Just a minute," I call as I hurry back to the table and praise the purple-and-pink butterfly arcing across the pale page, the orange-and-blue squiggles inside and outside the black-outlined squirrel.

I soak in these golden days of my nieces wanting my opinion, as I know it'll be no time at all until their peers' attention will be preferred.

I find it charming that they not only want my attention but that they ask so directly for it, without one drop of self-consciousness or guile. Then I recall that we adults do the same thing with updates, Tweets, and posts on the regular. *Watch me! Watch me!* scream our feeds … and we do. We do, until it's time for a social media break. Undoubtedly, mine is the first generation of grown adults willing to share minutiae my grandparents would have considered foolish or private —plated meals, outfit changes, car-interior or bathroom-mirror, fish-face selfies, you name it—with the entire world 24-7.

Discernment for what to share, how much to share (or how little), and when to share online are ongoing issues in our modern lives. There's no guidebook and no easy answers—just lots of trial and error along with learning about ourselves and from others' reactions (or lack thereof).

Similarly, as authors, we need our work to be noticed, yet there's no handbook or 100% right or wrong way to catch editors' interest. Still, there are tips that increase your chances of publication that I've found helpful in my 20 years of submitting work and that my writing students have used to acceptance letters in their own submissions that might help you narrow down which poems to submit for a submission call.

- **Put your best poem first.** You know that poem that has the colourful metaphors, the vibrant and specific diction choices, and the strong imagery? That one should lead the stack. **If you're not sure which poem is your best, ask a friend and/or your writing group to pick which one they like best and explain why.** Many literary journals receive *thousands* of submissions *for a handful* of publication slots (you read that correctly), so they might not read your entire submission packet—

knowing this, you need to put what you consider your best work first. **Once you've chosen your best poem, edit so that your first two or three lines grab the editors' attention amidst the sea of submissions.**

- **Include poems that cover universal themes.** Writing is an art form based on communication. Yeah, you might think initially that this poem is about your first bike and how you learned to ride it, so why would others care?, but **poems that cover milestones and common human experiences (schooling, graduation, parenthood, marriage, divorce, death, birth, learning a skill, moving across country, mistreatment, or falling in and out of love) have the potential to resonate with wide audiences. Make sure your approach to the topic is fresh and sheds insight on your specific experience**—and then step back as readers relive their own similar experiences through your poem.

- **Variety is the spice of a submission packet.** Most literary journals cap poetry submissions at either three or five poems per submission. (Always check the submission guidelines before collating your packet.) Knowing that you can only submit a precious few poems, it only makes sense to diversify. If you've included a poem about your dog, include another poem about your job or about that visit to Yosemite 10 years ago. Three topics, three chances to hook the editors' interest; whereas, if all of your poems were about your dog, you might get an editor who doesn't like pet poems (or dogs) and then your submission might be sunk before it was started. For general submissions of five poems, I try to choose poems with five different syntax styles, tones, themes, metaphors and similes, and/or characters.

- **Sometimes, linked poems are the way to go. Here's how to know.** I know this advice goes counter to what I just said a moment ago, and for good reason. Keep in mind that some journals *do* want poems that are part of a series or about the same topic (just like some visual arts magazines request linked work instead of individual shots that other journals love). The good news is that **journals who want poems that are related by theme or topic will almost always say so in their submission guidelines. Sometimes, they'll ask for poems from a project-in-process, other times, they'll want a chapbook of poems which means that the small collection must cohere** and make sense as a unit so that linked poems are not only welcomed but expected.

- **Match the types of poems the publication recently published to the poems you've written, including adjacent topics. Always read an issue or more of the literary journal you're submitting to or several of the chapbooks or collections from the poetry press where you're submitting manuscripts. Get a feel for the themes**

and voice styles of the publisher. What topics have they already covered? How does your work explore this theme but in a style that only you can create? If a few issues have included poems about the same topic, then make sure your poem has something that makes it stand out or covers new ground. Similarly, look for topics that might be adjacent to those the publication has covered. Perhaps their target audience is 20-somethings and you notice they feature poems about first apartments, but that they haven't published a poem about roommates in the past three issues— this might be your perfect opportunity to submit yours! Conversely, if the past few issues have had roommate poems, it would be wise to send your roommate poem to a magazine which hasn't already published poems on that topic recently.

- **Consider new venues.** Sure, we'd all love to be published by the big fish in the pond (How you doin', *New Yorker*! Greetings, *Poetry!* Salut, *Paris Review!*), but there are hundreds of literary markets in the world to choose from, many of which are grand ways to begin your publishing journey and to build a readership. **Submit work to new literary magazines that have just started publishing in the last year or less; they are often hungry for submissions and enthusiastic to promote your work.** What could be better? I've been published over 200 times, but I still submit to literary magazines seeking work for first and second issues whenever the posted guidelines interest me or seem to match my work. **Also, keep in mind that blogs and newsletters often seek poems.**

- **Play the Wild Card. I leave one of my poem spots for a poem that I consider either a game-changer or totally unlike the others in my packet.** Sometimes that means a poem I've written so quickly as to seem almost too easy and maybe not as edited as the others. Other times, that means a favourite poem that has been rejected before but which I still think has literary merit. Sometimes my wild card is a new poem I wrote that week or a poem that uses different syntax or diction choices than the other poems in my packet. Or it's a poem about a topic that interests me but that may not match my impressions of what the publisher publishes, but who knows? So I give it a try. The funny thing about my experiences with including a wild card is that about 60% or more of the time, my wild card gets chosen for publication over the other poems I thought the editors would choose instead. **Editors are only human like we are—with preferences and dislikes—and many times, they don't even know what they'll love until they read it in their inbox.** Sure, it makes sense to read the magazines or books and anticipate what editors may like the most, to match tone and themes with what they've published before, and yet: **leave a little room for serendipity and possibility**. **Round out a submission with a poem you personally like for your own reasons, even if it veers away from what they have standardly published and see what happens. You might be pleasantly shocked. For more dishy advice from editors themselves, check out Episode #8 of the Brevity Podcast, which is a jam-packed, insightful episode with practical advice from JoBeth McDaniel, Alexis Paige, Geeta Kothari, Tim Hillegonds, and host Allison K Williams.** *brevity.wordpress.com/2018/01/30/brevity-podcast-episode-7-submissions/*

- **Include work that has already received favourable comments.** It can be tough to narrow down one's own work. I often start with 10 or 12 poems, keep sorting until I'm down to six, and then narrow down to the final three or five. Especially as a beginning poet, **choose a poem or two which received positive comments in a workshop, class, and/or from your trusted readers (often friends and fellow writers or beta readers). These readers chose lines or stanzas that resonated with them for a reason, and the passages they loved may well resonate with editors, too.** If you don't have a beta reader or a posse of workshop pals, consider joining an online class or workshop (or starting one in cyberspace, your favourite café, or living room!) where you can meet other writers and provide and receive helpful feedback before submitting. (MA and MFA programs along with writing conferences and retreats are other wonderful ways of meeting verse buddies, but as they are rather expensive, not the obvious option for many poets.) Not only will you enjoy camaraderie and receive practice in receiving and giving feedback, but it will also make the journey easier once you feel it's time to submit your work. Before I had trusted poetry pals I could send my work to if need-be, sometimes I would sit and debate which poems to submit for over an hour; with practice submitting and knowing that I now have trusted lifelines in several creative friends for a second opinion, it usually only takes me about 15 or 20 minutes to choose my poems.

Try this Prompt!
Choose a literary magazine that
is currently seeking submissions.
Read their guidelines. Read two or three past
issues, to get a feel for their editorial style and
gauge what they've published recently (even
many print journals now publish a selection from
the current issue—take advantage of this opportunity and **support small literary journals
with donations, purchasing their publications,
and/or subscriptions**). Select eight or 10
of your own poems that you feel are strong.
Begin to narrow them down to three
or five poems, based on the above
guidelines.

Writer in Progress: The Writer's Idea Book, Submission Notebook, and You

Much of what we do as writers is onscreen. While Word files, attachments, and screenshots are excellent tools, one of the resources my writing students tell me they appreciate most is as three-dimensional and tactile as they come: the notebook.

In fact, there are two kinds of notebooks I often suggest to writers. The first: an Idea Book, commonly called The Writer's Notebook. The other: The Submission Notebook. I'll explain a bit about my process and recommendations for each, but **feel free to take these basic guidelines and bend, add to, or evolve them to suit your own personal style and writing practice.**

What are the advantages of keeping a Writer's Idea Book?

- You know those random ideas that hit you while in line at the market, in the middle of class, or while cooking dinner—those ideas are precious and fleeting. You think you'll remember them later, but you won't. Trust me: 99% of the time, like a comet tail, they leave a bright trail of *What was I going to write earlier when the deli called my number. Which was 17. Why can I remember the little scrap of deli paper and not my fantastic idea?! It was something about … um …* **When you carry the idea book and a pen, those random bursts won't pass you by again.**

- Here's the key, though: **make sure it travels with you.** It's no good if your notebook is always shoved under the backseat in your car or sitting on your desk while you're at work, at the park, or elsewhere. **A Writer's Idea Book should be as mobile as you are and connected to you.** Pretend it's your phone; most people have no trouble remembering to haul their devices everywhere.

- Unlike your phone, **your Writer's Idea Book won't beep, ping, update, or crash. It's the perfectly silent, always-available companion to your literary whims and wishes.** It'll also hold your place until you're ready to unleash your oddball creative genius.

What kind of notebook works best? Great question, that has about as many answers as there are authors and their personalities. Some general guidelines I've found useful in my writing practice:

- **Make sure it's small enough and light enough to carry with you.** I've seen some fantastic notebooks that were 8 x 10, had 300 sheets of paper, and were gorgeously rendered with leatherette covers that made my mouth water. But they had the weight of a brick. I don't want to cart around a notebook that'll knock my shoulder out of alignment, and since my writing notebook needs to be with me throughout my day, that's a no-go. Most of my notebooks are 5 x 7s with less than 200 sheets of lightweight paper.

- **I've found that wire or spiral-bound notebooks are easier to prop open on a desk while typing later.** This might not be a big deal for you, but for me, the fewer times I have to juggle like an octopus without the other six helpful hands, the better and faster I can type.

- **Pricier does not always mean better.** Yes, sometimes the bond of paper in a certain famous name-brand notebook is thicker, but for writing down those quick bursts, I personally don't care whether the paper is creamy or if the notebook cost me a dollar or 10. Most of the time, in fact, I buy notebooks at the dollar store or, if I'm feeling spendy, a discount department store. Sometimes, friends and family gift me notebooks.

- **If you're a visual learner or have big handwriting, consider unlined notebooks.** Some writers like to draw characters sketches or paste visual images beside their idea—if that's you, or if you have large handwriting as I do—you might consider unlined notebooks, or at least avoid college-ruled ones.

- **Some authors like to collage the front covers or to choose notebooks with motivational sayings on them.** If that draws you to the notebook, go for it. My current notebook that my five-year-old niece gifted me has a whimsical princess in a purple-and-white forest on the cover. The notebook before this one was a gift from a writing friend relocating abroad and included a Katsushika Hokusai painting called *The Great Wave, off Kanagawa* that spilled blue beautifully from front to back covers. These notebooks have personal meaning because of who gave them to me, but when I choose on my own, I pick whatever interests me in the moment. I've had geometric notebooks, striped notebooks, animal-themed notebooks, solid, one-hue notebooks, you name it.

How should I organize the inside of my Writer's Idea Book?

There is no right or wrong way to organize your ideas, but here are a few guidelines that writing students have told me have led to workable drafts:

- **Do a quick outline of your main idea. Include dots or dashes in front of each element in a list.** This is an idea, not the Sistine Chapel ceiling. It doesn't need to be perfect. Chase the gist now, and flesh it out with finer detail later.

- **Mapping, anyone?** Remember fourth or fifth grade where you wrote a word or idea in the centre of your paper, circled it, and then made this little spider-web-tentacle thing coming out in all directions from the circle? Yep, that's what it is. One thought after another, which you'll sort through and choose from later.

- **Write ideas on one page and leave the facing page blank, for later.** This technique is my jam. Seriously. I like to fill in the right-hand side of each notebook page and leave the left-hand side open for additional details that come to me later. I prefer room to expand, since my third-grade teacher made us skip every-other line in our drafts, in case we forgot a detail; well, I never had enough room on those single in-between lines to include the numerous ideas that occurred to me later. Leaving a whole facing-page blank reminds me that there's still plenty of room to play as I develop the idea and, like my third-grade drafts, takes the pressure off of knowing the entire work at one sitting.

How about a Submission Notebook? How do I organize it?

- **I recommend filling the information about your submission on one page and leaving the facing page blank as well.** In my own Submission Notebooks, I fill in a fresh right-hand-side page with information about each submission and leave the left-hand side pristine until it's time to write any notes about the submission, such as ink (praise, suggestions) an editor gave, a message that the original deadline has been extended, or details about publication from the editor.

What kind of information do I include about my submissions?

I include:

1. The date in the upper right-hand corner (it's scary how fast you'll forget when you submitted).

2. The number of submission (I number mine chronologically, since the first year I started making regular submissions which was—gulp!—2000). Some authors like to start their numerical system at the beginning of each fresh New Year or school year—there's nothing wrong with that system, it's just not how my own mind works. Use what you find most appealing.

3. The title of the market and kind of market (online or print, magazine or book publisher or agent, etc.).

4. The name(s) of my submission, including title(s), word count, and genre.

5. Any special information about my submission—if it's a simultaneous submission; the web address of the guidelines; if I sent it from my email account or an automated online submission service, like Submittable, that some literary magazines require; if I used a pen name. I also note if there's a reply time, which some websites will state and others won't. Sometimes I also record when and where the piece has been rejected before, especially if it's a favourite submission that's been rejected

a few time but which I still believe has a shot at publication.

6. I include little boxes at the bottom that I draw in myself. The left one reads: *Accepted*, and yeah, often includes a smiley face. The right-hand side reads: *Not interested.* Often, I jot a second or third magazine where I might submit the work if rejected, to motivate me to submit it again quickly.

7. I leave enough room at the bottom to record the dates of acceptance or rejection.

Why can't I just have one notebook for writing ideas *and* submissions?

- **The short answer: that's a jumble of information with two different purposes—one is creation-minded and the other is marketing-minded.**

- Personally, while I have to do both to be a successfully publishing writer, **I like a physical and separate tactile record for creation vs. submission as it helps me to feel more organized on each task at hand when it's time to do so.** Some authors might have no problem thinking of them both on back-to-back pages, but for most of us, I think it's handier (and more focused) to use separate notebooks. Go with what will make you feel happier.

- **I don't carry my Submission Notebook with me outside of the house—that's just a desk**

copy (I think of it as a reference book) that I used as a record of my monthly submissions—at least three, if not more. As such, **I usually only look at my Submission Notebook four or five times a month, compared to my daily contact with my Idea Book—yet another reason to keep them separate.**

Try this Prompt!
Take yourself notebook shopping.
You might want to start with a Writer's
Idea Book first and then pick a Submission
Notebook on another day, or perhaps you
want to buy both in one fell swoop; totally up to
you. You might want to set your ideal price and
style before you go/browse online, or leave it
up to serendipity and what the store has in
stock. Once you've purchased your notebook, begin the habit of carrying it with you
everywhere—and I mean everywhere—for a
week. Then add another week. And another,
until it becomes a habit. Watch as idea after
idea finds you prepared. Savour as note after
note becomes new poems.

Lavender Disappointment: On Poetic Adjustment of Expectation and Stalled Drafts

We'd talked about it shortly after I stepped off the plane in the Midwest. What it was going to be like, ambling through the lavender fields. The nectar-sweet yet spicy scent of the stalky purple blossoms. The many photos I'd take and maybe submit to a literary magazine. The muffins and brunch delectables we'd buy and share at the café afterwards.

"How cool! A lavender farm so close and so cheap to visit!" we said. "Usually, those are in far-away locales, like France." We agreed—at just 40 minutes away, it was practically in her back yard, and it was going to rock.

Sister found that the website said no tickets or reservations were necessary. That should, in retrospect, have been our first clue, but we set out that June day with high hopes and sunscreen.

Arriving there, immediately there was a snafu—Sister had to drive into what amounted to a ravine. Once in the ravine, there was a small sandwich-board sign— Parking Lot Full. To our right was a thicket of trees and a tiny dirt road not big enough to turn around in, to the left was the aforementioned parking lot that held maybe 20 cars if they were all compact and jam-packed—after you navigated down the one-lane dirt road that bordered the lavender field, which was five or six small rows on maybe an acre perched on a steep embankment.

Of course, nary an attendant or employee in sight.

I jumped out of the SUV and went to ask for further parking ideas from a stranger eating at the outbuilding that doubled as their breakfast café.

I excused myself and approached a lady about my age with dark hair and Jackie O sunglasses with her teenage daughter in short shorts who looked at me like I had four heads and all of them were disengaged from reality when I asked, "Do you know where there's more parking or even a place to turn around, because there're only trees in that direction and the sign says there's no more parking down there?" I pointed in the vague direction of the packed dirt-road lot.

"I don't think there is any more parking here. Just the few spaces below."

By this point, I ran back up to the SUV and informed Sister. We had two options: to sit and wait and hope one of the diners would finish quickly so we could nab their parking spot (although they all looked like they were in for a good, long nosh, given that the café was the only place to spend money *and* get out of the broiling noonday sun) or back out immediately, before anyone turning off of the road behind us pulled in and we would be trapped for who knew how long at the top of the hill.

A quick survey of the lavender—which didn't bring to mind the word farm and its expressive, rolling vistas, more like the circumference of the sandbox my dad built for me when I was still an only child in our backyard—and we decided we could live without seeing it. From the SUV, we were already seeing it—without paying admission, getting stung by the swarming bees, or the threat of, after finally spotting a parking spot, getting stuck later on coming up the hill of the one-way road as an oncoming car headed down the hill to try for a spot. No, thanks.

We strapped on our big-girl pants, heaved a what-are-you-gonna-do sigh or two, and went to a deli for sandwiches and soup—where the parking lot housed almost two rows of free, paved parking spots, none of them on either an embankment or a one-way dirt path.

So, it wasn't the South of France with dances through the rich expanse of acres after acres of lavender (that will have to wait until another year and when one of us makes a windfall), but it was still a meaningful time of sister bonding, nutrient talk and food, and more than a few laughs as we rolled with the punches.

Adjustment when things don't go according to plan is common while writing poetry. Expect it. Maybe you start your poem with one rhyme scheme, say a quatrain, and then find that there aren't enough words that rhyme with "fondant" that carry the meaning your lines need. Or perhaps you began with one theme in mind and then by line six, you realize you've spent five lines detailing an entirely different theme. Or maybe the draft that looked fine yesterday suddenly reveals itself to be facile and covering no more ground than dozens of other poems about this same subject. It happens.

Here are five steps for recouping with grace and renewed imaginative vigour when the best-laid poems go to the dogs.

- **What one line is the best line?** Pick that line (for its friskiness of language choices, its literary-device use, or the music of its syntax), get rid of the rest, and start the draft again to see where it may go.

- **Let your poem cool for a day or, if possible, a week or longer. Then reread it.** Pinpoint the spot where your tone changed or the poem repeated itself or went off track. Scrap the lines at that point and rewrite for 15 minutes from there until the end.

- **Does none of the poem seem to cohere? Are there a few phrases or lines that seem interesting or appealing, but together it's a patchwork mess of sutures? Pick multiple strands you like and throw away the rest. Then, draft a new poem from each individual strand you liked.** Say there were two phrases and three lines you liked. You now have five new poems in the works. You are under no obligation to enjoy all five poems, but odds are good that one of them will lead in a compelling enough direction to give your poem another chance for coherency.

- **Edit your poem over several days or longer. Understand that part of what makes writing different than most other pursuits is that you can have as many chances as you need.** Many, many poems begin at one spot and then, seemingly with wills of their own, veer off into left field**. You can use as much or as little of the initial draft as you want. Your poem can have 55 drafts over months if you want and nobody but you will ever know, unless you choose to share that information. Instead of focusing on the annoyance, remind yourself of the honour in writing consistently. Also, it's okay if a poem wants to be about something different than where it started—just go with it until the end of the draft.** Then, omit the first few lines and move other lines around the poem, adding connecting transitions, lines, or even whole stanzas as you shape the new material into a coherent whole. The process may take more than one sitting, which is also perfectly fine.

- **Do you have one hot mess? So all-over-the-place that you can't really say WHAT the poem is about or where you thought it would or should go? Get a trusted friend to read the draft and ask them, "What do you think this poem is about?" Offer no background and just listen,**

listen, listen. You may be surprised at what the person intuits from what you wrote. It might offer an entirely new idea that you hadn't thought of and can work into the draft. Or, conversely, the reader might have no clue what the poem is about or misread your work, and they may start to ask you what you meant by certain lines. If this happens, the worst that can happen is that you admit it was a free-write and you get some literary there-there and the joy of venting. Tomorrow is another day. There will be another poem and then another poem after that. **Save a copy of this poem, in case you get a brilliant idea for exploring it more on another day** (which can happen at the oddest times—for me, usually while walking or taking a shower). **Then move on. Some poems are just meant to give you practice,** to get you to the next poem(s) that will make complete sense. Like the lavender farm visit that wasn't, it's likely you'll get a nice lunch and some good chat out of the experience anyway.

Try this Prompt!
Pick two or three of these techniques the next time your draft oozes out of control. Which worked best?

76 Rabbits out of a Top Hat, or: The Quirky Tale of How One Poem became a Whole Book

Ever notice how some things just multiply? From one to many, seemingly of their own accord. Take weeds in a garden. Ants (or—eek!—roaches) in a cupboard. Emails in an inbox. Pounds on a despicable scale.

Or poems in a collection.

Yesterday was the release day of my poetry book. *This Passing Fever* (FutureCycle Press 2017) is a collection set in 1918, the last year of World War I. It was also the year of the influenza epidemic that took myriad lives the world over and tore some families apart while it brought other communities closer.

I say poems—plural—now, but it didn't start out that way. Originally, I wrote a single poem that I divided into three sections during the second draft. The poem was two-pages long and included three characters that, at that time, didn't have names.

So, what happened that I expanded the poem into

a whole series of historical poems? Here was my thought process and creative arc:

- **Stay open to surprises.** While fact-checking a detail in my initial poem before submitting it to a journal, I stumbled upon a jump-rope rhyme that kids used to sing on the playground in 1918. It was such an authentic detail that I immediately took it for a spin, exploring a question that jumped into my head and out through my pen: *What would be the life story of a girl singing this rhyme?*

  That new poem launched not only my main character, Alma Donovan-Smith, but a whole new impetus: *If Alma had a story to tell, what about other children in her school? What about the teacher? What about the students' parents? What about other people in the town, like the shopkeeper, the clergy, neighbours, and friends?*

- **Just because the work starts in one format or genre and length, no need to stay locked into place.** I ended up taking apart the initial poem and writing more poems about the villagers in a two-week period. It felt like they were individually introducing themselves to me. Of course, once I knew Alma, I wanted to learn more of her story, and she didn't disappoint. **Four or five poems in, the idea hit me to flash forward and listen as Alma told some of her own story, as part of an oral-history interview project with her grandson in 1958.**

If I had remained stubbornly determined that what I'd written was just one poem, what a loss it would have been to the narrative and to me! I learned a lot about handling multiple POVs and story strands in verse while dividing the pieces and omitting some that didn't work.

This wasn't the first time I'd used the take-apart and rearrange-while-expanding technique, either. In 2013, I wrote a three-page poem set in World War II, about an American widow and her son. This initial poem sparked my curiosity, and as I began taking apart lines to form smaller poems about my three main characters (Pauline, Edgar, and Charlie), more and more exciting details sprang to the surface. It was like I had picked up a phone that wasn't mine and participated in a Skype session to the early 1940s. Not only that, but once I started to follow the three characters' threads, I also flashed forward, much like I'd do later when drafting *This Passing Fever*.

I gave myself room to play, add, omit, and shuffle the details throughout a two-week period that led to the final manuscript of *Catching the Send-off Train* (Wordrunner eChapbooks 2014), published later that year. www.echapbook.com/poems/faith/

Feel free to take apart your draft, even after the last edit (as Walt Whitman did with numerous editions of his literary masterpiece *Leaves of Grass*). Add new details. Explore details you stumble across either while researching or that seem to find you as a gentle thought.

- **Go organic. Let the work inform your writing and editing decisions.** When I wrote the initial poem of *This Passing Fever*, I hadn't move back and forth through time from 1918. Yet, as I wrote more and more individual pieces and delved into both personal and cultural details of the town, I began to feel that a more-compelling way to present the narrative in verse was to fast-forward through several time periods.

Sometimes when we start a project, we have just the outermost glimmer of what the piece will become, and that's not only fine but magical. **Each piece will have its own innate format and logic. Stay aware and curious about the material as you write and edit. Respond as you go to how the piece moves and (re)shapes itself.**

So, instead of one poem, I have 76-pages worth … and a richer, more evocative exploration of my initial subject than if I'd stopped with the first poem.

Try this Prompt!
Poems and flash pieces are short by nature, but linked works have the potential to be significantly expanded in details, characters, settings, and more. Pull up a piece you thought was a one-off and examine it with new eyes. **Ask yourself: Where are possibilities to expand this narrative? What might another character say or do that could complicate the narrative and expand the conflict or tension? Try flashing forward or backward in time period or setting.** Take 20 minutes to write a companion piece to your initial draft (borrowing, omitting, adding to your heart's content), without stopping. You might just find, like rabbits out of a hat or chips from a bag, one leads to another and another and…

Keeping the Wolf from the Door: Careers in Poetry

My maternal Grandma Lou was one of the hardest workers I've ever met. She knew a lot about stretching nickels and dimes. Her father had died a few months before she was born the same year the stock market crashed, and she was an only child of a 39-year-old mother. Not only did Grandma Lou become a teen-age mother and raise seven children on a dairy farm, but her husband was frequently ill with kidney disease and she became a widow at age 39 with three of those children still at home (one of which was my mother). She went to work as a cook and waitress until her 60s.

By the time I was in high school, Granny Lou had a ruby ring (red was her favourite colour) with a prin-cess-cut stone that she bought herself that read "school of hard knocks" where other rings sport a university name. She still immeasurably loved her bright-red lipstick, trips to JC Penney once or twice a year to buy new shirts that she called "waists," and her black Shih-Tzu dog, Fifi Lou. Granny was stylin'. She surely wasn't lazy and she didn't abide by excuses from others: if things needed to be done, you were expected to see the need and pitch in. Despite bumps and bruises, she was also one of the most resilient and giving people I've known—when she won a microwave in a contest in the early 1980s when the technology was still pretty new, she gifted it to my parents despite not having one herself for several years after that; my parents used that microwave until 2005.

Grandma had a phrase, "that will keep the wolf away from the door." I like that phrase, although I seldom hear it anymore. The image of the wolf is potent in fairy tales as the harbinger of malevolence and ill fortune, waiting to burst through the door and lick its paws after a meal of carnage.

Melodramatic much? Oh, a tad, but then, the "wolf" is always panting at our own door as poets—**how in the world can I take a skill and an art form I love and make enough money from it to live when so many publications only pay bragging rights and a publication credit?**

The short answer is: you will need another job as you pursue your writing (which I also broke gently to one of my grad-school poets this week who was inquiring if "any poets make enough money to quit the day job to write full-time.")

The longer answer is: don't fret; it will all fall together as you keep writing and publishing, but yes, keep your day gig … and maybe add another gig on top of that. Few of my fiction-and-nonfiction writing friends and professors and none of my poetry peeps from grad school subsist on their "salaries" as writers, and these are long-publishing writers, many

of whom have either chapbooks or books on their résumés.

Let's take a moment to kvetch about this, shall we? I'm totally with you: I loathe that we writers—who spent numerous years of personal time, effort, thought, and money in travel classes, workshops, and sometimes, expensive grad schools and conferences—don't see real-world remuneration after such passion and sacrifice. In other fields, such as the sciences, business, and finance not to mention technology and the law, I'd easily make six to 10 times what I do now (if it stopped at that), in addition to insurance and full benefits, if not also a 401K, stock options, and educational reimbursement. (How I wish I could say "understatement alert," but alas, no.) The majority of creative writers I know have two or three part-time jobs or one full-time job and a freelance side-hustle and/or they also rely on contributions from other family members or roommates for finances. The cold fact of the matter is: **creative, artistic expression is unbelievably fulfilling (a silver lining!) and personally meaningful, but not a money maker.** [Cue the doom drums.]

This doesn't have to be a bad thing completely: day jobs give us a chance to interact with more people and have more in-depth, interpersonal life experiences. (It's not always all about the Benjamins.) Those oddball co-workers, lunch ladies at the local café, and conundrums at the water cooler do frequently provide the spark for writing a new piece and examining life more closely and outside of our own comfort levels.

Also, and please don't roll your eyes: living simply

and within one's means by only taking a maximum of one trip or getting one special/pricey treat a year, using belongings until they are completely worn or used, buying some things gently used, and paring down one's possessions to a few favourites rather than always buying new can be a freeing way to live with appreciation. I don't make much, but I always have new books arriving on my doorstep to satisfy my mind, and I value meals out and occasional splurges (like the fountain pen I bought two months ago) more than if I had several more zeroes in my bank balance or could afford the latest car.

Hey, many famous poets had day jobs. Robert Burns was a tax collector. Langston Hughes was a busboy. Lucille Clifton was a claims clerk. William Carlos Williams was a doctor (who reportedly delivered more about 3000 babies! Yes, that's *thousand.*), Frank O'Hara was a museum curator, T.S. Eliot was a banker, Anne Sexton was a model, and countless authors have taught. Several famed authors have held numerous jobs to support their writing, including Maya Angelou, who was a cook, calypso singer and dancer, actress, journalist in Africa, and the first African-American streetcar conductor in San Francisco. Walt Whitman was a government clerk, teacher, journalist, and nurse during the American Civil War. Charles Bukowski, although famed for being a postal clerk (which he wrote about in a novel), also served as a dishwasher, warehouse worker, gas station attendant, parking lot attendant, Red Cross orderly, truck driver, and elevator operator, to name just a few of the odd jobs he held. Why not join the illustrious ranks of the few, the proud, the working poets?

I hear you: "Okay, so if I HAVE to have a day job, **what are my options?** And make it writing-related, or at least writing-adjacent, please." **Here are some of the top careers for poets, especially if you have a Bachelors (or more) in English:**

- **Journalist.** Hey, you're good at collecting images and facts. You like to narrow information into smaller, packable content (you've already practiced that a ton with line breaks and stanza formation). Many newsletters for health organizations, small-town newspapers, and university- or college-quarterly brag mags desire write-ups by authors like you. Sometimes, you might be assigned as a stringer—journalist who is hired on a piece-by-piece basis—and other times, you might become a salaried employee who coordinates the article assignments, collates and assembles the articles using software, write content about reunions or campus events, or edit the whole kibosh. For the latter job, consider brushing up on your computer-software knowledge as well as looking into internships to get your foot in the door, or volunteer to write a piece or two to show your writing chops. If you've written for your school paper or have another, journalism-related clip or two, I'd consider writing a cover letter and pitching my services as a freelance writer. Guest blogging might also be a way to go before building your own theme-related blog and expanding to include advertising revenue in the future.

- **Ghost writer.** Does your publication have to be your own priceless baby? Nope. I've have friends who made beaucoup bucks from ghost writing another person's brainchild. **Consider it grand practice in organization, communication, and delivering on deadline.** You will still be creating another world. You will be handsomely paid for it, compared to publishing or posting your poems for free. **Two caveats:** you will not have you name on the cover, and you often will be restricted by a contract from telling anyone you had any part in it. For some authors, these stipulations are game-enders, and so be it. For others, it's kind of sexy to have a book out there that you wrote that no one else will ever know you penned, especially if you flexed your literary muscles in a genre you don't normally pen. **Freelance journalist websites and classifieds for authors, such as Poets & Writers, which has a Jobs for Writers section and a classifieds section, often list a few opportunities for those wishing to break into ghosting.** www. pw.org/classifieds

- **Freelance editor.** Love to read? Do you cringe when someone puts an apostrophe on a possessive its? Do you enjoy slashing away at adjectives and adverbs? Then this gig might be your bag. With the advent of online publishing, many self-publishing authors either hate grammar or have trouble spotting errors in their own work and routinely seek freelance editors who are self-

199

disciplined, enjoy helping tighten other authors' poetry or prose, and wish to set loose the most direct, beautiful diction the world has seen. In addition to internships (which are often unpaid but a great way to make contacts), if you've already edited a friend's or colleague's work, solicit brief letters of recommendation touting your skills and query publishers whose work interests you, especially targeting writing within genres that tend to publish at high volumes, such as romance and science-fiction publishers. Some publishers will require an editing test to double-check your skills while other publications will heartily assign you a first gig and then keep the assignments coming once you deliver the pen slashes on time. As a freelancer, you can take as few or as many assignments as time and desire will allow, and after you've edited for one publication and earned a good name, it's possible you will get more clients than you could handle at one time. Another good way to get started in freelance editing is to create your own website and network on social media. List your testimonials front-and-centre. Note your education and/or other traits that underscore your talents and passion for language. You can set your own hours and fees (wonderful perks!). You won't have co-workers, which could be good or bad, and you'll have to buy your own health insurance (which is majorly expensive and bad), but some authors are married to someone who has a health plan, and this is a non-issue for them. I take about 12 to 15 freelance projects a year, depending on factors such as the length of the authors' projects, if I'm writing a book myself, and how many classes I'm teaching concurrently. There are pockets of time where I have no freelance projects for three or four weeks at a time, and other weeks when I might have two projects I'm working on at once. **I would recommend editing for at least a few assignments with already-established publications before deciding if editing is a fit for you long-term.** Freelancing is flexible and sporadic, so you could technically give it a go while working another job, as I have done, since you won't always have many assignments at once. **Also, and this is essential: make sure to keep precise, organized records as you go (I recommend a spreadsheet or chart) listing all of your freelance gigs with dates and client information/email, as you will need to report your earnings to the tax man either quarterly or yearly and also may be able to deduct expenses such as print cartridges, depending on the employment laws where you live—consult your accountant for more information.**

- **Teach or tutor.** Yes, you knew it was coming, but honestly, of all of the writing-adjacent jobs I've held in 20 years, this one **inspires me the most and keeps my writing skills refreshed.** Teaching is a meaningful way to share what you know with a younger generation (or, in my case, with three generations: as I teach high-schoolers, early-to-mid-career professionals, and retirees, my students range from 14-years-old to their mid-40s to their 80s!) and to share some of your favourite works of art, depending on what subject you teach. (May I suggest English?) Sometimes, you won't physically be in a classroom building—remember: teaching now includes online as well as offline components or (as in my professional life) a split between the two. For a few years, I've taught both non-credit and credit classes online and find that both in-person and virtual writing-class students challenge, encourage, and motivate me and my writing life and enhance my skills as an instructor. **Just two big down sides: it's extremely poorly paying (no ching-ching here, I'm afraid) and teaching can be so engrossing and time-consuming that you have little time for your writing (insert frowny face). You will have to fight for time to write, either before or after school or on weekends or summers, but it's do-able if not always ideal.** Still, if you like the feeling of explaining concepts and meeting people from all walks of life and backgrounds and needs while developing a working understanding of the human mind as well as your own perceptions and misperceptions along the way, you can't get a better writing-adjacent job, no matter the drawbacks. **Make sure to give yourself some break times or sabbaticals. While teaching year-round (which I've done some years) can** be helpful financially, it can be an invitation to burnout, which doesn't serve the students or the instructor. Last summer, I scheduled early June through the end of July off from teaching to hang out with my nieces and read novels for the pleasure of it (oh, and to work on *In a Flash*, my book for flash nonfiction and fiction authors and also available through Vine Leaves Press). It was a meaningful, slow-paced break. When I returned to teaching and freelancing in the first week of August, I was refreshed and raring to educate again.

• **Small-press publisher.** This one works especially well if you are a go-getter, an extrovert with sales experience, enjoy networking and conferencing, and have (or are prepared to cast your net to get) several connections in the publishing world. **If you like matching authors and cover artists with eager readers and are enthusiastic not only about your own writing but others', the time has never been better for multi-faceted individuals who decide to launch their own online platform to bring works of literature into the world. I would highly recommend asking if you can talk to your own editor or publisher to learn more about the capital and time involved in their own business practices before leaping into the fray once you get a publishing credit or two..** If you're ambitious and creative (I know several small-press publishers who create their own cover art, which is another market-able—read: $$$—freelance skill), then it's well worth looking into as a possibility.

You might also combine some of these careers, as none of these careers is full-time (except teaching, although if you're an adjunct like I am, then that is also part-time). That said, here's something I might have told my younger self (although she was pie-in-the-sky and optimistic, so she would have listened politely and then done what she wanted anyway): figure out how much money you will need to live a comfortable lifestyle according to you, how much your bills might be a month, and take a class or earn a whole degree in a subject that is known to get that much salary or more. Set your expectations at the adequate level: **MFA, creative-writing money will never be MBA-level money, no matter how much education or how many publications you have.**

There is no shame in working outside of writing but pursuing it on the side: hey, it worked for Wallace Stevens, who spent his whole life at the bank, bringing in the cash, while publishing in some of the top literary journals of his day. He never had to worry about paying his insurance premiums, making his rent, replacing his car, or paying off student loans—his basic needs met, he could write his fingertips off to his heart's content with no extant debts.

The truth of the matter is: you might try one, two, or a combination of these jobs for a few years, switching off and on, or you might keep your gig as a cashier, senior-portrait photographer, architect, caterer, wildlife biologist, or accountant. It's also possible that the company or office where you work has openings that include writing skills you already have and may put to good use if you inquire and negotiate. **What matters most is that the job you choose leaves you with enough energy and peace of mind so that you can apply yourself with passion and determination to your writing.**

Listen to Auntie Faith carefully: if your day job is depleting your life of joy and focus, it will surely affect the quality of your art. If that's the case, it is likely time to pursue another vocation. On the other hand, make sure that you already have an action-plan and a steady income stream in place before you quit so that your imagination has plenty of room to romp and play without that pesky wolf prowling at the door.

A job can be in any field and still facilitate your life's needs, as long as it allows you a liveable salary (by your own standards) and the precious time and energy it takes to pursue your writing.

Try this Prompt!
Look at the five writing-adjacent jobs listed and pair each of them with skills you already have that would work well. Have you always been interested in one of them but not made the leap? **What one action step might you take this month to set the ball in motion?** For instance, might you ask for a letter of recommendation from the friend whose manuscript you helped to edit? Might you update your résumé or recent publication clips? Could you write a query letter? Might you ask around at the local newspaper or college communications office to see if they're hiring? Search online for ghost-writing gigs that might appeal to you? Network your services with friends or co-workers as a private tutor for students, so that you can have flexibility for your writing during other hours of the day? **Set a date, one month from today, to have that baby step completed. If none of these jobs appeals to you, no problem—either note what you like about your current job or describe another field that you believe would facilitate your needs as a writer and why.**

21st-Century Publishing & Guidelines for Finding Your Ideal Audience

Twenty years ago, online publishing was considered a short-cut or low-brow and a last resort at best. Ditto for self-publishing. Then came the social-media revolution of the late aughts (yeah, I still find that term a weird way to describe 2001-2009, too), which I teach about in my *English 540: Contemporary Publishers and Publishing* class. Happily, as we find ourselves set to rocket into the 2020s, the vast majority of literary journals—both university presses and independent publishers—have multiple social media accounts, web pages, and digital subscriptions available. Many publishers also have segued into publishing only digital content or publish significant excerpts of print content on their websites.

Gone is the stigma associated with sharing work online. In fact, some successful bloggers have turned their months of posts into successful books about subjects ranging from pets and motherhood to lifestyle and personal quests, from healthy living to overcoming obstacles they hadn't seen coming.

What does all of this mean for poets? If you want to be published, there are now more ways than ever to find your audience. Many methods—from publishing on Amazon to creating your own website, blog, or social-media page—are partially or completely free and totally within your own control.

On the other hand, it's not an all-or-nothing publishing world anymore. You may feel free to combine publication methods. You may still decide to submit to traditional, print magazines. Or you may submit to literary magazines online. Or you may start your own blog and/or website to post content (just don't double-post or simultaneously publish the same content on your own space and via a literary magazine at the same time—that's considered a no-no). Or you may use social media to combine writing with another artistic discipline, such as photography or painting. Or you may decide to try several or all of these methods concurrently. The sky's the limit.

As you build your readership, here are some questions to consider that will help you to decide which types of publishing may be best for you and your work. Consult these guidelines on a project-by-project basis, exploring the needs you and each project may require.

- **How often will I post?** Daily? Weekly? Monthly? When/what time of the day will I schedule to blog? What type of poetry will I post? All of my own work? Will I solicit my friends' work to showcase and be open to guest bloggers from time to time? How will I find others interested in guest blogging?

- **Will my blog or new literary magazine focus solely on poetry or other genres as well?**

- **Does my target audience include people I already know?** Co-workers? Students? Fellow artists in my circle or school? People I've yet to meet? **What is my target audience's approximate age, educational or artistic background, and interests? What themes or ideals do we share in common? How would my target audience like to hear from me—via video or Skype, through short bursts of information (such as posts or Tweets), with craft articles that have tips (such as on a blog)?**

- **Do I feel more comfortable beginning an online readership with a like-minded literary partner or group, where duties can be shared? Or do I like having complete control of my literary platform and have time and energy to dedicate to the platform consistently?**

- **Am I comfortable sharing early drafts that are possibly unedited with my target audience? How much, if any, editing will I do before posting? Will I set settings to allow comments or feedback on my work? How might I feel about receiving comments/feedback?**

- **How much time will I dedicate to replying to**

comments or submissions? How much time will I dedicate to interacting with my readers? Will I schedule breaks to avoid burnout and for writing rejuvenation offline?

- **How much, if any, of my work will I submit to literary journals or other markets that I don't personally control?** How long am I willing to wait for a reply from editors/staff? Does my work match best with a small literary journal or a larger one? Does my poetry match best with new literary markets which may have a higher acceptance rate or with long-established markets which might accept 1% or fewer of their thousands of submissions?

- Keeping in mind that many literary journals want unpublished work, which means work not published online before in any blog or site, **how will I decide which pieces I want to submit for possible publication to outside sources and which pieces I want to keep for my own blog, social-media account, or other publication method?**

- **Does any of my writing feel too private to share?** Is there some work I would rather wait to share or share with a restricted audience, such as only close friends?

- **How much time, money, and energy do I want to spend on sharing my work? How much time, money, and energy will I realistically spend**

on sharing my work? What tiny changes may I make in my schedule to create a match between my answer to the first question and my answer to the second?

- **How comfortable am I marketing my own work? Who is in my network and how might they help spread the word about my work? How might I help others spread the word about their work?**

- **Would I rather spend more time writing and less time publishing and self-promoting, teaming up with literary journals or publishing professionals who will share the work but might change the editorial content or focus of my platform?**

- **How much time will I dedicate to my writing this week? How much time will I dedicate to publishing, submitting, and/or marketing my work this week?**

Keep in mind that there are no right or wrong answers to any of these questions, and each author will feel comfortable with their own combination of personal and/or external publishing methods. You may also choose to adjust your answers to these questions at any time and throughout your writing career.

Try this Prompt!
Spend an hour answering the above questions. Which answers surprised you? Which answers helped you decide the method(s) for reaching your audience? Make one tiny change in your schedule this week and schedule that new free time with more attention to your submissions, publishing your own work, and/or marketing your work.

Spring out of a Writing Rut! Eight Tips for Getting Back to Business

At first, it seemed exciting—you've always needed to write poems about your grandpa's sailing adventure or your childhood, and now at last the floodgates have opened! Huzzah and high-five! Then, soon enough, you realize: *Uh-oh. I've used this same phrase in four of the poems, and, wait a minute! some of the same imagery recurs, too.*

Whether you've written 10 free-verse poems in a row with the same theme or 100 pages with characters and plots that go around and around the same old scene but don't seem to advance, we all get into writing grooves at one time or another.

We've all been there. **It makes sense that writers have certain pet themes that we try to explore. The problem is when we've explored the same ideas time and again from every conceivable approach and our work begins to sound the same or ceases to take us in new directions on the page.**

If we're honest with ourselves, we pretty much

know when this is starting to happen. Likely, you had the spark of a first line, but instead of racing to jot this bon mot into your writing notebook, you took your time beginning the draft. Or while writing you find yourself running out of steam and stretching for something else to say, especially from the mid-point, or for a way to tidily end your draft. Or you finish your draft and have a let-down feeling, like you haven't accomplished much and aren't excited about working on the draft anymore.

Try one or more of these eight tips when you find your drafts part of a too-often-trod path.

- **Switch genres.** If you've written many poems lately, try a flash-memoir piece. If you've been writing exclusively fiction, write a poem. Instil a sense of play, seeing how an old idea can become renewed when working within a new container.

- **Read something unrelated to your theme or poetic style.** In fact, if you're interested in another art form, such as knitting or photography or dance, pick up a magazine or peruse your favourite blog online. I got the idea for this chapter from a photography magazine I read that offered specific tips for stuck visual artists (but nary a suggestion for authors—*Bingo!* went my brain). Many arts can inspire reinvigorated writing. I love interviews with makers of all sorts, describing their work and revision tips and tricks, struggles, and inspirations along the creative path; Google or YouTube search some interviews or find tips in your favourite blogs.

- **Make a "spark inventory" of people, places, and/or things that you don't know much about but find interesting.** It could be that you've always wanted to know more about the Amish or Bollywood, or how people become pastry chefs through Le Cordon Bleu, or what it's like to live in Muncie or Madrid or Montreal. Pick one or two items off of your list and peruse the internet, e-books, tactile books at the library, or other sources and take notes of anything that makes you slow down and go "hmm." Schedule a research trip. You'll recognize that inward tickle as it sparks. Keep your notebook or laptop handy.

- **Repeat after me: "No more writing about _____, until I've written three unrelated drafts of something else."** Write it in a sticky note and hang it near your laptop or on your phone if you have to. It's amazing how making one restriction can frustrate the Muse into rerouting to a new topic.

- **Give yourself a small rest.** A day or two to rest or even just a pause of a few minutes can refresh the mind and stir ideas. **"Small" is key; don't let the break stretch into weeks or months. Write, even if it's not your best work,** but do take some breaks if writing nonstop has dried the well.

- **Take an action break.** Go for a walk, bike ride, swim, hike, exercise of your choice. Get moving and watch new ideas percolate with the motion.

- **Call or Skype a writing friend.** Ask what your author pal does when a writing rut hits. Commiserate, swap ideas (and this chapter), and agree to meet for a free-write in person (or online) soon. Schedule while still online. When next you meet, do a 15-minute free-write and then, at the stroke of 15 minutes, stop to share and offer comments, then write for 15 more minutes and share. Repeat as often as you want.

- **Try writing in a new place.** Sometimes, new sounds, sights, and smells can trigger us out of ruts and into a new perspective conducive to innovative ideas. **Writing at a different time of day may also do the trick.**

Try this Prompt!
Make your own spark inventory. The next time you find yourself in a rut, you'll be all set to pick one of the topics, perhaps do some research, and get writing again.

Section III
Maybe Think
of Me Once
in a While:
The Poetic Life
and Identity

Tough Times, Tougher You: Writing about Adversity

"SURELY ALL ART IS THE RESULT OF ONE'S HAVING BEEN IN DANGER, OF HAVING GONE THROUGH AN EXPERIENCE ALL THE WAY TO THE END, TO WHERE NO ONE CAN GO ANY FURTHER." —RAINIER MARIA RILKE

It could be a cross-country move or a relationship that dead-ended without your understanding why. Or maybe it was the car accident or the death of a pet or a school you didn't get into or a promotion you were passed over for (again) and it still hurts. Whatever it was, from small slight to life game-changer, you've been through it. You've suffered, wondered why, and felt like you'd never smile or play or be carefree again. Until, one day long after and little by little, you did.

We're all survivors of something … usually multiple disasters and disappointments. "Everybody has a story," my mom likes to say, meaning we all carry the patched-over emotional and/or physical scrapes and dings that come from being human, and we live onward after trials and struggles.

These wounds are fantastic sources for poems and prose. With a little vision and a lot of bravery, they can offer a large portion of your material. **There are several types of poems in particular that mirror the agony of human experience** and which provide excellent containers for your personal circling through Dante's nine circles.

If sorrow is your head-on subject, **you can't go wrong with the elegy.** Sometimes known as a threnody or lament, this poem directly addresses or is in memory of someone who has died. When President Lincoln was assassinated, Walt Whitman penned poems in the deceased leader's honour to help work through the nation's shock and melancholy along with his own. You might also think outside of traditional lines and write about the loss of a golden period in your life, a favoured belonging irreparably broken, damaged, or lost, a hope that died so that something else could happen (although it certainly didn't feel like it at the time).

Consider the aubade. Two lovers part in the morning. Something ordinary sizeable has come between them. In the case of Shakespeare's star-crossed teen lovers, w*hole families.* For some inspiration, try Louise Bogan's "Leave-taking" or Kenneth Patchen's more oddly exultant parting in "As We Are So Wonderfully Done with Each Other." While these poems may also carry a cheerful tone of the newly besotted, a bittersweet twinge and a woeful resistance to separating also resonate well with the subject of overcoming emotional adversity. What do the lovers celebrate, even while parting? What agonies of loss will they carry with them, whether throughout years or just a single hour until reunion?

For layering personal traumas with cultural or artistic ones, you might try an **ekphrastic poem**. Based on reactions to a visual piece—such as a photograph, painting, architecture, or sculpture—ekphrasis is a lively and meaningful way to critique, reject, describe, or dramatize personal and communal pain. William Carlos Williams among others wrote poems inspired by Pieter Brueghel's painting combined with their own unique vantage point and experiences, whether directly in imagery or more indirectly in tone. In our visual culture where posts and websites are loaded with snapshots and visual art, the possibilities for ekphrastic sparks are as endless and individual as our fingerprints.

For use in writing poems about obsessions or frustrations that take great effort to overcome, **take a whirl with formal styles, such as villanelles and sonnets**. Their strict rhyme schemes and patterns of phrase repetition lend themselves well to the kind of cyclical misery-go-round many people have experienced with bad habits or in tragedy's aftermath. Dealing with the death of a loved one is another frequent theme for formal poems, as in this poignant sestina by Charles A. Swanson, which also explores gender expectations and the heavy burden of grieving a parent.

"Man-Up: Preaching My Father's Funeral"

My father taught me how to be a man.
I still remember what it felt to suck
gasoline. Lips on rubber, I drew breath
until the oil-sick sweetness gorged my head
with fumes, then I spat—the pull, up and out
to start the flow from tractor tank to ground.

It was my mistake, so I had no grounds
to argue. Dad's quiet words commanded.
I had unhitched the red gas hose, pumped out
the wrong fuel into the diesel. I sucked
the gritty tube. The smell went up my head
right away. I sucked deep with strangled breaths,
tried to will my gut and brain not to breathe.
Gravity favored me, the waiting ground
was below the tank. I quick-bowed my head,
prayed to siphon. I had to be a man,
I had to find an inner strength to suck
it up so I, at last, could suck it out.

Another time, I bottomed plowing, walked out
to find Dad. He plodded with me, his breath
labored. I remember how he had to suck
for air. "How could you get stuck in dry ground?"
he asked. War-hardened, not much fazed this man,
but his heart attack had. He scratched his head,

seeing the tractor's angle, the headlights
pointing to treetops, front wheels jutting out
of the dry grave I'd dug. He demanded,
"How did you do this?" I gulped a small breath,
said, "I plowed deep." The Tidewater ground,
low-lying sandy land, seemed to suck

me in. The grave had taken the plow, suckled
it on an unforgiving breast. Ahead
of me lay a long job, moving the ground
with the shovel Dad found me. I dug out,
spade by spade, all by myself. It was a breadth
of continent to move. But I was a man.

When Dad died, sucking all fight out of me,
I was buried head-deep, gagging for breath.
Ground turned to quicksand and I sank, unmanned.

Formal poetry also often expresses the height of emotions with first-time experiences or, as in this Italian sonnet, a tender ritual shared as a rite-of-passage between father and son.

"Love Shaving"
by Charles A. Swanson

I push the button on the aerosol can
and white foam billows like a scented cloud.
Our son appears, his eyes arched in a wow,
seeing magic cupped in my left hand.
I trace my stubble, feathering my coarse stand
of red with white. And with one finger plow
a straight line along his chin. He stands proud,
a bearded boy, ready to be a man.
Alone, looking in the steamy glass
I feel your touch pillowed in shaving cream.
You have moved into the silk-smooth stroke
of razor on my jaw. Your fingers pause
on the soft skin left behind. It's like a dream.
I'm still a boy, despite my beard and luck.

Care to read more formal poetry? Dylan Thomas' "Do Not Go Gentle into that Good Night" is an excellent reference point. His defiant tone and directive to fight until the last drop of light is a classic falling-down-a-thousand-times-and-rising-once-more call. Rita Dove's "The Cane Fields" and Theodore Roethke's "The Waking" are other meaningful examples.

Reflecting on strings of circumstances and experiences that led up to or through the hoops you had to jump? Why not try **a list poem**? This form is at once incredibly personal and communal. The imagery in your groupings may shed light on the specific times, places, conflicts, and emotions your readers have also survived. This kind of poem also tends to give readers a more grounded, well-rounded view of the topic you're exploring.

Much like formal poems although without the strict rhyme pattern, **the prose poem** may be used to employ artful repetitions that underscore the heavy, seemingly unmoving burdens in life. Repeat a particular image, phrase, or bit of dialogue several times to maximize the tension and emotional impact of events and circumstances. Russell Edson's quirky prose poems are searing examples to study this form.

Try this Prompt!
Pick one of the six suggested poetic forms
detailed. Draft a poem about an adversity
you've overcome. Pick another poetic form
and write about an adversity you're still working through and how it's felt via specific,
sensory-laden imagery. Go!

Repeat after Me: I *am* a Writer: Beyond Playing Identity Dress-up

One of my favourite subjects to ask students about is their start in this writing life. **When did you first realize you were a writer? Who or what encouraged or discouraged this identity?**

As an educator for half of my life so far, I've heard heart-warming tales of parents (like mine) and pals (ditto) who encouraged my fellow writers to keep writing and seeking publication, despite mountains of rejection slips, mounting student debt, and a cold shoulder from the outside world. On the flip side, I've been told agonizing stories from writing students about how their parents or partners pressured them to pick a more stable, sensible career (understandable, at least from a salary standpoint) and, in some cases, refused to help fund their education or even ask about their writing (gut-wrenching). I've been heartened to learn that some of these same students returned to workshops or masters programs 10, 20, or more years and several career detours later, more determined than ever to pursue writing, no matter the obstacles or cost.

The first time I realized other people viewed me as a writer as much as I viewed myself as a writer was in 11th grade. Our English teacher, Mrs J, assigned a project where we interviewed classmates about our talents and then gave a speech about our classmates' responses. To my surprise I was the first person chosen, by my friend, B. I was not used to being first pick. True, I had a small but close group of pals, but when it came time for sports' teams, drama tryouts, or other, more outgoing group pursuits, I was drafted in a late-middle round at best.

My friend seemed honestly interested in my writing process, how I created characters and dialogue, and my writing goals. Dutifully, B recorded my answers on lined paper. As if I was an expert!

How many pages was my latest story? Did I want to be published? I remember him asking. This was 1993, before internet publications, back when SASEs were the only way to reach editors and you had to go to a library to get a physical address and a name of an editor from a writing magazine masthead to know where to send the writing. Quite a process (compared to now), but yes, yes, I did plan on being published.

To my surprise, I sounded (and felt) respected for what I was privately pursuing. Glancing around the room, no one else seemed to be having as good a time nor staying on-topic, like we were. For everyone else, the assignment was an extra study hall. Strands of conversations about soccer and basketball practices swirled while the rest discussed parties, hook-ups, and break-ups, and the usual high-school gossip that clotted the halls.

Before that project, I had no idea that my passion

for writing would be recognized by other people and I'd never sought attention for my writing; it was just something I loved doing and was determined to keep doing until a nebulous someday far in the future when, maybe, my books would appear on a shelf somewhere. How would it happen? I still had no idea, but I had the motivation to keep pursuing until it did.

After that project, I realized that there were other people who believed that, with my skillset and personality, I was a writer already. What a game-changer for a scrawny introverted nerd with a depth-perception problem that would go undiagnosed for years; it was a needed confidence boost, to be sure. Several times in the years that followed, as my work garnered rejection slip after rejection slip, I returned to that interview in class and how sure I'd felt answering B's thoughtful questions. It was enough to reaffirm what I knew about myself and my writing. It was one of many positive reinforcements that kept me persevering.

Whether you've published or not, whether you've studied writing formally or are self-taught, whether you would ever list *writer* on your tax forms, you are a writer in your own right. When you introduce yourself to a new acquaintance or co-worker, throw in the phrase "I also write." Schedule regular time two or three times a week to prioritize writing new projects or editing older work, just as you would pencil in doctors' appointments and family vacations. Write *I am a poet* 20 times in a row in your journal or until it sinks in if you have to. Join a writers' group or start your own small coffee klatch or workshop once a month if the encouragement of others pursuing the same craft gets you going. Whether people acknowledge your writing publicly or you jot in a journal that you hide under your pillow and no one ever sees, **begin to claim writer as *your* identity.**

Try this Prompt!

What are some of your acknowledged identities? You're probably a cousin, uncle, nana, mom, in-law, co-worker, friend, or neighbour. What are some of your lesser-known skills? You might be a firehouse volunteer, a chocolate-chip cookie baker, a gardener, a rock climber, a philatelist, a woodcarver, a pack rat, a knitter, a neatnik, a resident grouch, or a yard-sale enthusiast. Who first made you aware of this trait or pursuit being part of what people think of when they think of you?

Pick one of your identities. Write a piece exploring either the pros or cons of this identity **OR** another identity you would pick if you could be your own public-relations expert, either now or in an earlier stage in your life.

It could also be interesting to write about a secret identity few, if any, people know about you. A humorous tone might be the way to go.

Singing out the Body Gift: Verse of Physicality

I awoke out of a deep sleep at 2:16 am. One minute zonked out, the next: eyes open to the TV I'd left on. My body groggy, confused, and yet entertained by what I noticed on the flat screen. A ballet was on the public TV station, but unlike any I'd seen before. It was an adaptation of *Carmen*, performed without lyrics.

Instantly, I was riveted. I've been a klutz for most of my life and I've never taken a formal dance class, but the way the young dancers used their lithe bodies to tell narrative was a revelation and inspiration. The emotions their bodies expressed through fluid, molten movements, the way they contained space and moved across it! To be able to move like that, recreating an old tale and making it entirely, excitingly new with hands, feet, torsos, and eye movements!

Tumble, drip, coalesce, part, recombine, arc, swirl, sweep, fold, unfurl, unfurl, unfurl. How active and amorphous, each a separate body yet representative of every person encountering love and struggle through the ages!

They were so syncopated and perfectly timed, like

watching the machinations of a clock work, I forgot that it was so early. The lead, portraying Carmen, was the only dancer wearing a sleeveless, graceful black tunic; all other performers wore white, sleeved, floor-length shifts or (for the male dancers) loose white shirts with white flowing pants. Not only that, but the sets were super simple, focusing even more attention on the nuances of the dancers' bodies in motion: just a black screen or curtain and white-painted, large wooden semi-circle platform, and an orchestra playing the original score. To watch the dancers move was almost to forget that they were flesh; to remember was to be astonished all over again.

I am reminded: unlike professional dancers, few of us believe we have this kind of physical fluidity and poise. **Many of us have a fraught relationship with our bodies, low on self-acceptance and high on wish-listing. We punish our bodies for not being tall enough or short enough or thin enough or shapely enough or healthy enough or athletic enough or muscular enough or xyz enough. Or we struggle to reclaim our younger selves or our pace in the aftermath of illness.**

I read a stirring article last week in a magazine that profiled women who had had double mastectomies. One of the warrior women had her scars tattooed with the most seamless, gorgeous blossoming lanyard of blooms, a riotously lovely symphonic dash splashing down and up her torso. Between these teenage dancers, who I was fortunate enough to waken to, and the article and accompanied black-and-white photos of the profiled cancer survivors, **I think again of the body** as a landscape that's not only personal but unifying. Not only singular, but a collective art-form.

Few poets have sung the mystique and strength of the body—both female and male—better than Walt Whitman. In the second section of his paean to physicality, "I Sing the Body Electric," Whitman proclaims:

> The love of the body of man or woman balks account, the
>   body itself balks account,
> That of the male is perfect, and that of the female is perfect.
>
> The expression of the face balks account,
> But the expression of a well-made man appears not only
>   in his face,
> It is in his limbs and joints also, it is curiously in the
>   joints of his hips and wrists,
> It is in his walk, the carriage of his neck, the flex of
>   his waist and knees, dress does not hide him,
> The strong sweet quality he has strikes through the
>   cotton and broadcloth,
> To see him pass conveys as much as the best poem,
>   perhaps more,
> You linger to see his back, and the back of his
>   neck and shoulder-side.

The sprawl and fulness of babes, the bosoms and heads of
    women, the folds of their dress, their style as we pass in
    the street, the contour of their shape downwards,
The swimmer naked in the swimming-bath, seen as he
    swims through the transparent green-shine, or lies
    with his face up and rolls silently to and fro in the
    heave of the water,
The bending forward and backward of rowers in row-
    boats, the horseman in his saddle,
Girls, mothers, house-keepers, in all their performances,
The group of laborers seated at noon-time with their
    open dinner-kettles, and their wives waiting,
The female soothing a child, the farmer's daughter
    in the garden or cow-yard,
The young fellow hoeing corn, the sleigh-driver
    driving his six horses through the crowd…

Without shame, without doubt, turbo-charged imagery in each line! Whitman is a lover of life in its infi-
nite variety and expansion. That gorgeous phrase "the
sprawl and fullness" says it all and is expressed in the
chock-full, inclusive lines—acceptance and celebration
in its tone, in the music of that phrase, and in the imagery of all types of people, with many vocations and
occupations from laborers to mothers to swimmers and

babies and everyone in between. One not praised more than another. One not rejected in favour of another. Each body is blessed and beauteous in his lyric.

Two of the best poems I've ever read in celebration of a woman's body are "Phenomenal Woman" by Maya Angelou and "homage to my hips" by Lucille Clifton. Don't let another day go by without reading these gems.

How seldom we praise our bodies and truly appreciate their amazing ongoing functioning, as Angelou and Clifton do so splendidly! I admit, in all of my teens and 20s and well into my 30s, I would instantly zero in on what I disliked and what disappointed me about my body—I wasn't tall enough, all of the weight I gained went to my abdomen no matter how much exercising I did, I was hairy, on and on and on. How often I catalogued my perceived flaws. It's only been in the past few months after turning 40 that I've been able to chip away at the language of that self-rejection and flipped the script: to approach first and foremost what I savour about my body. Even to admit to myself that there *are* things I savour about my body—it's a step toward deeper amazement and appreciation for life in a wider way. It's a work–in-progress, but it *is* progress.

Perfect, Whitman maintains. *Perfect.*

"The Body Gift"

The beauty in the fan of feathery
lines at my hazel eyes
when I share cool cups of laughter,

slender ovals
of my fingernails, graceful
half-moons across a page

I fill with a flurry of language
from my mind into another's lips
speckled snowflakes of accumulated speech,

two muscled, strong legs
stretched across a chair, in a dapple of sunlight, legs that twirled in kitchens with nieces

to exultant music, proceeded up graduation platforms,
legs that led me into the warm arms
of a returned but not forgotten friend.

This body:
gift not soon enough
unto its self.

Many writers have claimed physical exercise assisted their writing process. Authors as diverse as Louisa May Alcott, former United States Poet Laureate Kay Ryan, Don DeLillo, Andre Dubus, Haruki Murakami, and Joyce Carol Oates have credited running with inspiring their writing process. Kurt Vonnegut walked in his neighbourhood, swam in the local pool, and did push-ups and sit-ups. Novelist and poet of the collection, *Gravity,* Elizabeth Rosner swims. Novelist Beth Hahn is a dedicated yoga teacher and practitioner while fellow novelist Vanessa Manko is a trained dancer who likens her writing to choreography. Henry David Thoreau once noted "the moment my legs begin to move my thoughts begin to flow." Whatever kind of movement gets your heart pumping and your brain boosted will assist your writing journey. Keep both mind and body active and engaged, and watch your poems pirouette, pas de valse, and plié.

Try this Prompt!
Write a poem in praise of your body. I know—it can be tough or feel weird, like boasting. It took me four times longer to write the above poem than it did to write and type the notes about the dancers. No matter: if it's hard to get started, first write this poem about what you admire about a love, a child, or your best friend. Easy, right?
That was your warm-up. No excuses. Flip the script. Write the poem about *your* features next. If you need another pair of eyes to notice anything praise-worthy—no judgment, we all have tough days—ask three friends what they think is your best physical feature or quality. Prepare for the compliments! Begin your poem with those three physical traits.
Go!

For Further Inspiration, try:

- "My mother's body" by Marge Piercy www.poetry-foundation.org/poems/44882/my-mothers-body

- "Her my body" by Bob Hicok www.poetryfoun-dation.org/poems/49231/her-my-body

- "The Author to His Body on Their Fifteenth Birthday, 29 ii 80" by Howard Nemerov www.poetryfoundation.org/poems/42707/the-author-to-his-body-on-their-fifteenth-birthday-29-ii-80

- "Mother and Child, Body and Soul" by Jean Valentine www.poetryfoundation.org/po-ems/43184/mother-and-child-body-and-soul

- "A Body Drawn By Its Own Memory" by Kate Col-by www.poetryfoundation.org/poems/53645/a-body-drawn-by-its-own-memory

- "Body & Isn't" by Bruce Covey www.poetryfoun-dation.org/poems/54383/body-isnt

- "Body Builder" Cathy Park Hong www.poetry-foundation.org/poems/53602/body-builder

- "Body and Soul" by Sharon Bryan www.poetry-foundation.org/poetrymagazine/poems/41522/body-and-soul

- "When the Body" by Linda Hogan www.poetry-foundation.org/poetrymagazine/poems/88743/when-the-body

- "Body" by Alissa Leigh www.poetryfoundation.org/poetrymagazine/poems/41697/body-56d21ff4585f1

- "One Body" by Natalie Scenters-Zapico www.poetryfoundation.org/poetrymagazine/poems/92044/one-body

On Tenacity: Six Tips for Increased Poetic Productivity

One of my favourite artist retreats has a fascinating podcast. Makers in many genres, from fibre arts to writing, photography, and pottery, are interviewed in a one-on-one conversation about their creative lives, how they make time for their art, life-work balance, their favourite themes, teaching and/or their small businesses, and how they get their ideas and develop them.

Recently, a painter discussed her journey from high-school graduate in a corporate world to going back to college as an adult with grown children. As she described her personal renascence while pursuing her bachelors and the excitement of being in a community focusing on personal cultivation, she discussed an assignment for one of her courses: to make 16 paintings in four weeks.

Wow. That's four paintings a week. I've never been a painter, but I've known a few and that's a brisk pace, to say the least, especially when even commissions can take weeks if not months.

Then, I started to think about it further, in relation to my own creative process. Yes, it's a lot of work, but on the other hand, all artists learn through practice. Not willy-nilly practice, but diligent and ongoing practice.

The best way to get better is not to get precious about the work, especially in the middle of making it. That's one of the reasons why when I was an MFA student studying poetry 12 years ago, our groups were assigned a portfolio of new poems to workshop with our fellow grad students each month. A funny thing happens when you get an assignment to turn in eight or 10 new poems month after month—you start to pick up your pace and adjust.

Were they perfect, publishable drafts? Mostly not, but that wasn't the primary goal of the assignment. Writing that many poems, you begin to sharpen self-editing skills and also, from making comments on others' drafts, you teach yourself ideas for your future poems. You learn that the only way to increase your skills is to work consistently, so work-flow habits become attuned; portfolios written a few hours before deadline were likely not going to impress or make much sense.

One of my favourite professors told us, "What you learn in this poem might not help this poem, but it will undoubtedly be used in service of your next poems." That only works if you are routinely creating so that you're prepared when inspiration strikes. Keep creating. Preferably a consistent and large body of work.

That's one of the reasons I recommend to my own writing students that they take part in writing challenges. **In April, for National Poetry Writing Month, poets across the world take part in a daily challenge, writing a single poem a day. Some poets form groups**

or do informal swaps, as I've done, with poetry friends to encourage each other through the 30 days of the challenge and to share drafts. **I highly recommend swapping work with writing friends as a practice that increases motivation at any time of the year.** Even if you can only swap once a month or a few times a year, just knowing someone else is waiting for your latest work is enough to coax the Muse into motion.

Six Ways Poets Stay Motivated:

- **Drafts don't have to be perfect. Realize that good enough is great.** Ever hear the aphorism "Perfect is the enemy of good?" If we seek perfection, it's likely we'd never write. On the other hand, a terrible first draft is material to work with and may be polished into a stellar poem through several edits. When in doubt, just begin: write something. It doesn't have to be beautiful or remain the first line or first stanza forever (or even in the poem at all). All parts of a poem are malleable, but if you have nothing on your page or screen, there's nothing to work with—and that's the real shame of sporadic writing.

- **Get into a routine.** You might pick a time of day. Perhaps at 3:30 am, before your kids need to get up for school or before you begin your daily commute (I've had writing students who have done both). Or maybe you're a night owl who likes to write once the house is asleep and you're clocked out of your job(s) for the day (works well for me). Or maybe you designate one day your writing day—say Tuesday. Any time during that day, sit down to write. Or maybe you take a writing challenge—agreeing to swap work with a friend once a week or daily during NaPoWriMo. Write the challenge and/or the swap day in your day planner or online calendar—it's a deadline to meet and should be regarded as sacrosanct as paying your taxes (ugh) and going on vacation (ah, yes!). Experiment with days, times, and ideas that work best with your schedule and commitments.

- **Speaking of vacation, replenish your batteries from time to time. Realize when it's time for a rest.** It may seem counterintuitive, but all writers need some breaks. I call them "replenishing the well." Whether that means a few hours or days, some of the best writing can come after a day off to take a walk, meet a friend, or just lounge with a magazine or book. Give your writing (and your mind) blank space to breathe. Peruse older drafts for new material once you're back into the groove of your writing routine. Before you take your break, make a plan for the next day you'll write to ensure you'll have an idea in mind and motivation to return to your new project or draft-in-progress.

- **Read a lot of poetry.** Peruse your favourite poets' work (for me, a perpetual go-to is Mary Oliver) and find new favourites in literary magazines, both online and off, and at sites like The Poetry Foundation (www.poetryfoundation.org/), which has a searchable database with poems of almost every theme and style you can imagine.

- **Find a writing partner to trade work with, join a workshop group (or start one), or take part in a writing challenge (or set up one of your own).** If the monthly NaPoWriMo challenge doesn't work for your schedule, agree with a friend to write a poem every day in November (which also has just 30 days) or another month that will work for you (a friend and I are currently doing a daily October poem swap), or agree to send each other poems daily for a week of your own choosing.

- **Return to older/earlier drafts. That's viable writing practice, too. Have several poems going at once.** I do this with many writing and photography projects. It works especially well since it's hard to edit or properly judge a piece when it's freshly created; once the rose-tinted goggles have cleared a few weeks or months later, I return to edit earlier poems and photos, especially on a day when I'm not sure what to write.

Try this Prompt!
Write a poem about your writing
process; these are called *Ars Poeti-*
***cas.* For some inspiration, check out Sha-**
ron Old's "Take the I Out," Billy Collins'
"Workshop," John Brehm's "The Poems I
Have Not Written," or Galway Kinell's "The
Bear." Then, go ahead: get friendly with your
writing, what it means to you, and how it
interacts with your daily life. Personify all
you want; maybe your Muse wears a bright
pink feather boa and has a raspy, comedic,
Phyllis Diller laugh or perhaps your writing
mojo is a counterintelligence spy who speaks
four languages and wears a black shirt and
Raybans, blending in seamlessly in a crowd
of passersby. Throw in some alliteration and
fanciful allusions to describe what it's like
for you to write and maybe even what
keeps you struggling to write what
you want.

On Attention

It happened yesterday. I was in the middle of talking about lunch plans and when I glanced down at my arms, I noticed a dappling of tawny-coloured pin-prick-sized freckles on my arms, just above my elbows. I stopped.

"Wait. When did I get freckles there?" I asked aloud and then laughed. How quickly I'd forgotten about sitting on the porch two nights last week near sunset with a stack of magazines and a novel.

Life has a way of unfolding so fast that it sneaks up on us when we aren't looking while racing from class to class or obligation to obligation. Our bodies, our thoughts, and our opinions are constantly shifting. Many jobs now require huge swathes of online content—from blogging to social media to web sites to increased marketing and networking—as part of their requirements. More and more distractions enter our private lives, too—from constantly texting or sending emails to movies, music, and other entertainment endlessly streaming on our devices. Even the word "devices" suggests an influx of information and a removal of attention from things right in front of our faces. I'm as guilty of this as anyone.

Part of the poetic job description is that **we are artists who notice. We slow down and focus on the details, experiences, and circumstances that others shrug off or blast past.** Although our cultural pace and online obsessions aren't likely to change any time soon, **here are some small but significant ways to return to a life of noticing. Try them and watch your writing flourish.**

- Impossible to have a cyber-free week or even a whole day due to deadlines? **Take a disconnected afternoon. For a few hours, leave your phone and e-reader at home. Leave the house for a park, café, or other spot. Repeat after me, "I am in no hurry."** Pack an old-school notebook and favourite pen to record any thoughts or ideas that flit through your mind. If nothing does, that's okay, too—live in the moment and record what you noticed later.

- **Take a walk through your neighbourhood and observe.** Take 20 or 30 minutes to avoid looking at the screen. **Make it a habit to look around more, to notice** the dogs, neighbours, vehicles, and flowers in your own little corner of the world. What has changed? What is the same? How have you changed this month or year or decade? Think about how you are also the same. **Record your impressions once you return home.**

- **Challenge a writing friend** to notice three specific details about their home, office, neighbourhood, or city today. You will each sit down and pen a poem including some of the details you notice and email or (better yet) trade poems in person soon. Set a deadline; **deadlines are pixie dust and make things happen.**

- **Pick a time of the early morning, early afternoon, or late at night that you can commit *solely* to your writing.** You will not, repeat after me—*not,* use that time for taking a peek at your inbox or answering just one text that will turn into ten. Your focus for 20 or 30 minutes will be taken completely and only with your observations and writing. **Buy a program that will lock the internet for a specific time if you have to. Get an accountability partner to check in and keep you on track. Choose a lovely notebook that will invite you back again and again.**

Try this Prompt!
On Pinterest (ironically and of all places!) there is a meme with glorious green trees that reads, "There is no Wi-Fi in the forest, but I promise you will find a better connection." Today, you are going to live that meme, strictly for research purposes, of course. Try one of the four suggestions above as part of your writing practice. Even better, pick a day each week for a month and try all four. Which one yields more poetic inspiration for you?

Write Opportunity, Wrong Timing

"But it was such a good fit! It perfectly matched what their guidelines said they wanted!" Oh, the rejection slips I've received, many times multiple in a month. Honestly, it's all part of a regularly writing author's life, though no less annoying and hurtful.

Haven't we all encountered the right opportunity, wrong-timing dilemma? It's the worst. Similar to finding out you're a runner-up for a job you won't get (happened to me, twice) or that you were second (or third) choice for a friend's lunch halfway through the meal when they admit so-and-so was busy (open mouth, insert fork). To say nothing of the seemingly endless landmines of right idea, wrong timing in love and dating.

Yet, we proceed and stumble through with the resiliency we didn't think we had. "The only way not to get rejection slips is not to submit your work. And you shouldn't not submit your work because of rejection. Rejection happens to all writers. No exceptions," a wise professor once told my class. Truth. But no less easy to stomach, as all writers know or quickly learn.

Tips for dealing with rejections and making proactive steps forward beyond "Thanks, but this work doesn't fit our needs at this time."

- **Give yourself a few hours to process the annoyance.** Rejection is awful. You're entitled to feel what you feel. Being published once is no guarantee of future success: writers who have been published numerous times still get rejections and are hurt, understandably so. For a so-funny-because-it's-true take on rejection, read rejection tales posted online, including Alexis Paige's hilarious "Rejection Sucks and Then You Die: How to Take a Dear Sad Sack Letter (And Shove it)" at *The Rumpus* and "Famous Authors' Harshest Rejection Letters" by Romy Oltuski at *Flavorwire*.

- **Don't dwell.** Easiest thing to say, hardest thing to do—but, please, do yourself a favour and get busy doing or thinking about something else. Anything else. Don't knot yourself into a ball for weeks about their vague rejection. Please *don't* email the editor for an explanation; that's a free ticket to an ulcer and a bad name among editors. Whatever the reason was, and you'll likely never know, the work was rejected. That doesn't mean it wasn't well-written or innovative or worthy of publication. It means that one editor at one magazine passed on the work, that's all. Move on to a new piece of writing or another publication. Which brings me to:

- **Submit the rejected work again, within a week.** I mean it: find another market or, even better, make a list of three or four magazines for work *before* you send it the first time, so that your back-up plan is in order and you don't second guess yourself when rejections happen. You'll take a few deep breathes, feel scuzzy (that's allowed) for a few hours (no week after week of obsessing), and then, you'll send it out as another submission packet as you get busy writing another piece.

- **If you get a line or two of ink that suggests why the market didn't accept the work, as you sometimes will (especially as you get close to publication-level writing), consider that feedback.** If there's any sense to it, kudos—open up your piece and edit according to the free tip you just received from a wise editor. If, however, the response doesn't make sense to you (it happens, not all editors are well-qualified or have the best intentions for your work) or doesn't appeal to you, check with a writer friend or someone else to see if it makes sense to them. It's always your piece, so you don't have to change a word if you don't want.

- **Pep talk and treats.** Google stories of how many times famous writers were rejected—they abound on the internet and, in truth, amongst all publishing authors I know. Treat yourself to something you've wanted for a while—whether tangible like a new pair of shoes or a cheat meal or intangible but no less wonderful, like a long soak in the tub, an afternoon movie with a good friend, or an hour reading the fascinating new book you just borrowed. You've acknowledged the hurt feelings, now soothe them a bit.

- **Begin to see publishing as a numbers game.** If you're math-averse like me, just typing that sentence made me cringe, but hear me out. My most successful writing friends—the ones who publish small pieces a few times a year or big projects every few years and have a consistent readership—are the ones who also receive the most rejection slips. That makes no sense—initially. Then you start to realize: they receive more publications *and* more rejections because they are writing more *and* submitting on a more-frequent basis than sporadically submitting writers. Who is more likely to receive more acceptance letters—the person who submits to two literary magazines a year or the person who submits to 40 magazines a year? I submit at least three publications a month, often more. On a good year, I've submitted up to 60 times, of which I'll receive rejection slips around 45 times … but that still gives me 15 publications for the year—more than that two-magazine submitter accomplished.

- **Diversify.** Who doesn't want to be published in *The New Yorker* or a similar big name in the literary-magazine world? **There's definitely nothing wrong with aspiring to greatness out of the gate—go for it! On the other hand, if you only ever submit your work to the glossy trade magazines or well-known university magazines, you are cutting off opportunities at magazines that receive far-fewer submissions each year**

yet have the same thing the powerhouses have: readers! Most literary magazines, even small ones, have at least hundreds of readers—respectable and worthwhile. I suggest that my writing students choose small, big, *and* mid-sized markets *as well as* new literary magazines that are untested yet actively seeking new work—the latter of which have been some of the most motivated, enthusiastic supporters of writers I've ever met and a dream to work with before publication.

Look: the wrong timing is terrible, miserable, horrid, and rotten. I hear you and totally agree. **Rejection is unsavoury and there's no way to make it a joyous occasion. Then again, you face the pain and come through it knowing you did the best you could with the reality you had. Keep writing and submit again.**

Try this Prompt!

Remember that piece that was rejected months ago? The one you believed in until the *no thanks* crushed your dream, so it's now parked on your hard drive? Exciting news! It's calling your name and ready to rumble … onto another editor's desk. Today, you're going to find two markets to simultaneously submit it to (check guidelines to make sure the markets accept simultaneous submissions—most do as long as you note it on your cover letter) and then, you're going to submit to them by the end of the week. Next week, you'll find another two markets and submit the piece again. Then, you'll begin a new piece of writing. Consider yourself assigned a deadline! Go.

Dealing in Disappointment Without Wielding the Hatchet: Calming the Confessional

We've all been there: we sit down to write and who should appear but the bevy of bellicose jerks both large and small who've stepped on our last nerve. The bitter bark of your in-laws sniffing about how they never let their kids stay up that late. The registrar who skipped you when assigning classes and never explained nor apologized. The frenemy who flirted openly with your date over dinner. The relative who made the snarky old-maid comment. The snide paper-delivery person whose aim got even worse once you called to lodge a complaint. **In a profession where "write what you know" is common advice and which makes perfect sense, why shouldn't we let off a little steam now and again?**

- **For each fault of someone else's that you note, your credibility lessens.** How much do you enjoy the non-stop griper who unloads vitriol while sitting down next to you at the dental office when all you want is to sit quietly with your book and nervous stomach? Readers may take one or two details about the "one who did you wrong," but soon, the spotlight will turn to you. What about *your* faults? What part did *you* play in what happened or at least in how you chose to respond? Or did you hide/stay silent? What are *your* Achilles heels? These questions make more compelling literary reading than a diatribe against someone else or a group of people. Whining does not make compelling reading. I recommend first writing the diatribe for yourself and your own clarity. Then, begin anew where you address your own part in this scene or problem—this is the draft you will show to your writing group and/or writing friends for suggestions, not the rant.

- **Readers may understand the type of person you're annoyed with and why, but they prefer the vulnerability of a writer who admits their own weaknesses, struggles, questions, and quests.** Readers don't have to want to be your best buddy, but they should be on your side enough to want to keep reading your poem. If your work is a screed of scathing anger, connection will be hard to sustain, and readers will tire. **For every fault of someone else's you bring to light, bring to light one or more of your own.**

- **While some readers may enjoy your confessional poems, there are many readers who want deeper resonance or who don't want backstage**

passes into your personal life. Yes, the Confessional Poets of the 1960s, including Robert
Lowell and Anne Sexton, had a huge following and blasted back the doors of polite society
to show a tender, rotting underbelly for others
to acknowledge. Yes, these works were ground-
breaking and important to the development of
more forthright, modern poetry which took the
commonplace and made it communal. Still, it
has been over 50 years since this revolution in
poetry subject matter. 100% autobiographical
poems have had an audience long enough now to
become almost, dare I say it? (because I do enjoy
them—well, here goes), commonplace. Consider
these questions as you edit: **What makes my poem's details bigger than just my own life? How
does my experience connect with or enrich the
struggles my reader is going through or has already survived?** If your poem is a laundry list of
how you've been wronged as an individual in a
rotten situation, it might be time to rewrite to
increase your scope and resonance.

• **While we, of course, bring our own life experiences and disenchantments to our work, if the
sole purpose of the poem is to seek validation
or prurient interest in our own lives, then the
poem will backfire.** Instead, I recommend to my
students (and to myself, because I admit I've written quite a few navel-gazers) that they **switch to
third-person and inject fresh details into the**

poem. **Perhaps you will include a fictionalized detail or two so that the poem becomes about something deeper and more universal to your readers than just gazing into the rarefied terrarium of your troubles. Or maybe you will change the point of view to the person whose snark most grinds you.** Or it could be that you challenge yourself to change so many details that no one would ever guess it was you and the inciting incident becomes merely that.

- **Certain emotions are collective to being a human: frustration, dashed hopes, longing, anger, or hanging-on-for-dear-life and subsequently starting to let go. These are the emotions your poem's diction choices, line and stanza breaks, and speakers would do well to explore.** Get your grumbling and grunting out in the first draft if it helps you to clear the way for a poem that will connect with your readers' experiences and deliver a "me, too" through your own admissions.

- **Let some time pass.** Not many of us write clearly or eloquently about fresh experiences, especially in a first draft. Nor can we fairly judge how our prose may resonate with readers in the flush of inspiration. It's nearly impossible to edit immediately following a first draft, either. Give yourself a few hours, days, or weeks to get some perspective, and then return to your draft to see if any of it is vindictive, self-indulgent, or (one hopes) universal to human experience—edit accordingly.

To a certain extent we all write about what we know and there's nothing inherently wrong with it on the surface. Still, when poem after poem becomes a "why me?" poem, it's time to take a different approach. **Not that your poems should go full-tilt Pollyanna, roses, and sunshine—that would be off-putting and artificial.** It's important to write about life's unfairness but use the above tips to broaden the scope of your poems and to temper your work. **The negative is so much more rich and evocative when underscored by the tender and vulnerable places we shield.**

Try this Prompt!
Go ahead. Get the diatribe out onto the page or screen. There, feel better? Just warming up? Okay, but set that draft aside. You're going to write a new poem with just one line from the old one allowed. All other details in the poem have to be new. Challenge yourself to change POV and diction choices and to include a fictionalized detail that will flesh out the poem's scene or happening. Watch as your new poem blooms from personal grudge and pain to human complications and connection.

Sparkling Stone or Peach Macaron: The Trying-on-a-New-Persona Exercise

I have a thing for nail polishes. I love their hues, their genie-lamp-esque curves in tiny glass bottles with wand applicators, or their shiny, matte, or glittery finishes. My nieces, too, are gaga for a good polish, whether pricey or dollar-store bargain.

I especially love their names: Sparkling Stone (my current shade), Peach Macaroon, Sweetie (a rich earthen brown shot through with silvery spangles), and Lemon Pie (inexplicably cinnamon-heart red). Two more bottles "accidentally" made their way into my shopping basket this morning with the bread and lined-filler paper.

I can't wear mascara on my stubby eyelashes. The times I've tried (even with the supposedly hypoallergenic or clear mascaras), it's scratched my eyes and eyelids to distraction (ditto for most eye-shadows). Yet another reason I enjoy the transformative pick-me-up of a bottle of vernis à ongles. Rare is the week when I don't polish my fingernails a handy shade and give them a topcoat to extend the life of the lacquer.

Such a simple ritual, but an evocative one. If I'm feeling sedate, I gravitate to hushed tones of pale pink and barely-there beige. If I'm feeling particularly energetic and creative, I brush on a glittery turquoise or neon pink. If I'm feeling (or want to feel) outgoing and strong, it's va-va-voom red or sleek maroon (what is now often called by the ominous moniker *oxblood*).

Trying on a new polish (or even an old one, I keep them for a year or two in a long, woven basket) is akin to trying on a new identity. Who do I want to be today? How will this shade broadcast something I'm feeling but not verbalizing? Will this shade put a spring in my step or gently reassure me that I am meaningful as-is?

As with my nail-polish beauty ritual, it doesn't take much to coax a perception change. Even subtle perception changes are a gold mine for writers.

In our writing, we should always challenge ourselves with new techniques. Like athletes, we should expand our boundaries, even if with incremental goals. Do you always write haiku? Try another formal form, such as a villanelle. Even a free-verse poem. Or how about a short story or flash memoir? Are you well-known for your pithy style? For once, get all up in there with verbosity. Have you mostly written fiction because it was easier to get a character to voice what you've always thought? Today, you'll write as the speaker of your own tale in a poem.

It doesn't matter if your piece feels like a fraud at first (*But I never write memoir!*) or an awkward duck (*What's a scene without my beautiful adjectives? This just isn't right.*). You don't have to write in this genre or style long-term. It's not a mortgage; you're not locked in. Give it a whirl, and (if you must) retreat back to your comfort zone tomorrow. First, take that tiny step. Go ahead, venture into new territory and see where it takes you.

Try this Prompt!
Add a simple accessory to encourage a shift in your writing style and perspective. Try penning in a fancy silk scarf or special-occasion tie, a keepsake ring or outfit that once belonged to someone in your family, a hat you seldom wear, or your five-dollar sunglasses (my sister and I often joke that cheap, five-dollar sunglasses will survive the apocalypse but any pair more expensive than five bucks will get lost seconds after sitting them down anywhere). Some authors borrow or buy new clothes. One of my writing students once admitted to wearing a slinky chemise under her boring work uniform on days when she wanted to write, to get the creative mojo moving at the thought of her secret. Still other authors go shoe shopping for an infusion of oomph. Pick your props to suit yourself.

But it needn't be about clothing or jewellery: simply pick a different location, a place where you've never written before or rarely go to write: in your washroom or basement, the new café that opened across town, that fourth-floor nook in the campus library near the Zoology section, the stairwell of your apartment or dorm (all kinds of interesting things happen in stairwells, according to my undergrad students, but those are stories for another day).

Your goal today is to make one or more outward changes in how or where you present yourself in order to crack open new written territory. Bring your notebook and favourite pen—or borrow one as your prop of pizzazz to see what new territory it covers. Write from the POV of a character who is decidedly not you or note how you feel differently in your skin with the accessory or new surroundings. Any memories or sense perceptions that arise are welcome.

Playing a (Not-So) Simple Game of "I Die" in the Backyard

"HAVE PATIENCE WITH EVERYTHING THAT REMAINS UNSOLVED IN YOUR HEART. TRY TO LOVE THE QUESTIONS THEMSELVES, LIKE LOCKED ROOMS AND LIKE BOOKS WRITTEN IN A FOREIGN LANGUAGE. DO NOT NOW LOOK FOR THE ANSWERS. THEY CANNOT NOW BE GIVEN TO YOU BECAUSE YOU COULD NOT LIVE THEM. IT IS A QUESTION OF EXPERIENCING EVERYTHING." —RAINER MARIA RILKE

While watching the darling nieces so my sister can get one of her first non-interrupted showers in months, they shriek and giggle from swing-set to fire pit to the little patio closet where all of the backyard furniture gets stored when the wind howls.

"Catch me! Catch me!" They call to each other. "Watch me! Watch me!" They yell to me, then to each other as they dangle, swing, and run. I offer praise on their strength, their speed, and their playing together kindly, and then sneak peeks back into my chapter from time to time.

My younger niece, Sylvie Ro, suddenly drops to the grass.

Immediately, I gaze up from my novel, scoping out

the potential damage, figuring (as the more adventurous of the two) she'll likely not cry unless she's fallen on a spike or something is horribly mangled.

She's smiling good-naturedly and fine, just as I expected, but what she says next amazes and amuses me in turn.

Splayed on the grass like a two-and-a-half-year-old snow angel in the sun, arms akimbo, her white-blonde hair mad-scientizing in every direction, she whispers to her elder sister, Cora Vi, "I die." Immediately, she lets her tongue loll to the right corner of her mouth and clasps her eyes closed.

Our Broadway actress, I think, suitably impressed. *Yale Drama School, here we come.*

Cora Vi, a newly minted five-year-old, finds Sylvie Ro's behaviour hysterical. She giggles buoyantly. In her ultra-girly flower-print sundress, Cora Vi stands over Sylvie's motionless body and gently taps her painted toes by Sylvie Ro's hands as if to jolt her, while both erupt in more laughter.

Where did they learn this? I wonder, as they switch places. *Resuscitation by laughter,* I chuckle to myself.

My elder niece takes her turn, running and then plunking her body onto the grass at a random spot. Dainty, Cora Vi's death splays involve far less gusto but no fewer giggles from both.

I smile. I can think of no less life-affirming sound at that moment than two healthy little girls, thoroughly entertained, and (for the moment) not squabbling or angling for toys and territory. Their imaginative play and self-amusement, quirky and harmless and, frankly, humorous. Their game continues, unvaried and unbroken, for 20 minutes—one dropping, one standing in a sundress over the body of the other, gently tapping, poking, or leaning into the other's face brimming with laughter, the "deceased" springing back to life like Lazarus.

My nieces are not alone. Many of my friends who have had children comment on their kids coming up with similar games, seemingly of their own prompting. I recall that odd, old game, "London Bridge is Falling Down," with its lyrics about ashes falling down; it wasn't until I was in my teens that I learned the real origin of those ashes was a reference to the Black Plague bodies. But young kids tend to be fiercely pure and unselfconscious about life's more demeaning or demanding experiences. They address questions aloud in an earnest way and often believe that there are meaningful answers for conundrums and mysteries.

We live in a world abuzz with fertile questions about stages of life, career, relationship, and overcoming grief, sadness, and adversity, you name it. **As poets, raising questions is also crucial, even when (perhaps, especially when) we are unsure of answers, if there are answers that would satisfy, or if we feel certain there are no answers we can understand. Countless poems begin with a question that the poet has been pondering for days, months, or even years. In fact, whole books of poems have been written exploring crucial questions,** and Pablo Neruda even wrote a volume announcing that facet in the title: *The Book of Questions.*

While the question may not be directly stated in

the poem, this seed of curiosity as it searches to grow in meaning might be nurtured into the rich ground of theme, tone, or plot. Forget self-consciousness or "haven't a million other poets before me tried to write about this experience, loss, or pain? What could I possibly add?" Asking questions can be a key growth experience as a writer. Push through. Ask on the page what you've always wanted to know, what you've been exploring for years, what you hope to know for sure when the answers resist knowing and remain a mystery to be coaxed.

Today, try to love the questions themselves just a little bit more, especially in a brand-new draft.

Try this Prompt!
Either write a poem about a game you recall from childhood and its more-adult meanings that you now realize as an adult but didn't at the time **OR** write five questions you're still pondering and choose one as the theme for today's draft. Go!

On Purposeful Play

One of my favourite hashtags—you know, those quirky, thematic word combinations with the # symbol that social-media posts include to hook readers—is **#doitfortheprocess**. Thousands of crafters, professional artists, and hobbyists use this hashtag while sharing their works-in-progress. In fact, a newsletter I received recently said that 474,000 posts include this hashtag every few hours! That's a boatload of creating going on.

Many of these people only posted their highlight reel, so to speak. These were the pieces that they consider successful, while they hid the stumbled starts and stops. Yet, each piece is an important part of being a maker. Much like inventors such as Edison who, according to legend, took 1000 tries to invent the light bulb, there will be many, many imperfectly executed ideas or false starts; **as inquisitive creators, though, none of the time, effort, and fun is wasted. Each piece leads to another and another piece, refining and exploring as we go. Consider all writing an experiment. Meet the idea without judgment and see where it takes you.**

I've been publishing in literary journals since 1999. While I submit at least three submissions of poetry, prose, or photography a month, I create vastly more writing than I ever submit. Yes, you've read that right (as you hold the heft of this book that's like a door-stop of productivity)—I have way more writing on my SanDisk than I submit. Why? One of the many reasons is that **sometimes, the pieces are just play. Like musical scales,** I like to riff and see what I can make out of thin air and the random spark of inspiration. They are for the fun of exploring an idea. **Or they begin but need time to gestate. Or, they are a start that leads to a better piece later on a related (or even unrelated) topic.**

Too many times, as writers, we expect anything we spend time on to lead to publication or at least a finished piece. We get caught up in the production trap—if you don't have a finished piece then aren't you a failure? Maybe that's the analysis in industries and sales, but **in creative writing, the attempt and the process are just as—if not even more— important than the final outcome.**

Will people think of me as less of a writer because much of my writing is still on my computer and not in the world? Not even close—they won't even know. What they *will* **know is that I've written a lot over the years, and how will they know that? They will feel it in the pieces that I do release to the world,** the pieces that were birthed as a result of the many hours I spend writing and revising per month, the hundreds of hours of penning just for me as well as for my target audience.

Only as adults do we insist on creating with the intention that it becomes something, a finished prod-

uct. Children create for the joy of creating. They do not consider assessments, what we adults might label as publication, awards, money, or publicity. Whether nobody sees it or a whole auditorium does is of little interest as they focus on play.

The process itself may be a long-awaited breakthrough … or it may come to nothing. One of my little nieces made a drawing and midway through, she decided she didn't like it. Crumple-crumple in her fist and she immediately turned back to her blue-lined notebook, picked up her purple marker, and set to work on another depiction, her pink tongue tip sticking out as she concentrated on drawing concentric circles.

I noticed that she didn't dwell on the crumpled piece on the table beside her. She didn't try to explain what went wrong or what she didn't like about the original depiction. She didn't bemoan the state of her skills or call herself talentless. She didn't think she had to have it all figured out before she started or why bother. Nope.

She calmly flipped to a new page and got started again.

Try this Prompt!
Let's emulate our favourite children and our fellow inventors today. No fuss, no self-criticism, no doubt. For your new project, don't bother with setting a goal or a deadline. If it takes you five hours or five years—who cares? Don't begin the creation with the idea of sharing, but if you end up sharing later, feel free. In the meantime, delve into the spark of an idea and see where it goes or if it goes anywhere. Follow blind turns and random connections. Go ahead, #doitfortheprocess.

Top-10 Tips for a Sustained, Inspired Poetic Life

"I WOULD DEFINE, IN BRIEF, THE POETRY OF WORDS AS THE RHYTHMICAL CREATION OF BEAUTY." —EDGAR ALLAN POE

- **Write the first few drafts for yourself. Later, edit with an audience in mind**, especially if you are planning to share your work at a poetry reading, slam-poetry event, workshop, class, or literary magazine. Remember having fun? Don't underestimate the joy of getting lost in the process … and then found again in the editing stage.

- **Compress it!** Omit prepositional phrases, adjective pile-ups, and repetitions (unless it's a refrain or part of a formalist poem). Consider where lines and stanzas end and begin: are those the best places for breaks, the places that highlight solid diction choices and key themes?

- **When in doubt, include imagery. Even if not in doubt, specific images are the way to go**. Aim to include at least some of the five senses. Remember that authors tend to overuse sight imagery. Why not include an auditory image? Or a tactile image this time instead?

- **Consider how small poems might fit together into a larger submission, chapbook, or collection.** What themes do the poems share? What kind of narrative arc might several poems in a row share? Conversely, are there some longer poems that might be divided into smaller poems, emphasizing a theme and omitting details that are redundant or unnecessary? You can also write new poems that would fit in with a collection idea once begun.

- **Read other genres from time to time. Read poetry consistently.** I love reading novels, memoirs, and essays. Many poets read across genre lines, and that's wonderful—all writing has the potential to inspire the Muse. Just make sure to read your own genre often as well. Peruse online databases of poetry, support and buy collections of publishing poets both online and at readings, and read your friends' latest poem drafts while you share yours. Fill your mind with a profusion of poetry, and then watch for the verse waterfall.

- **If you want to write a poetry book, start getting poems published in literary magazines where you can collect an audience or develop an online presence** where you consistently share your work *before* approaching a small or university press, an indie press or contest, or self-publish. In my English 540 Contemporary Writers and Publishing course, we have six or seven assignments that ask students to analyse the target market or target audience of their work. That's no coincidence. If you want to publish your work, ask yourself who your ideal reader is and then match that ideal reader to the readership of small literary magazines you read. You can get a sense of the ideal readership by the poems a journal publishes. Don't just read one issue—study three or four, and then jot down your impressions. Match your impressions with the poems you've written or will write soon.

- **Don't write because you feel guilt-ridden that you haven't written in a while** (we all feel that way sometimes); **write because it's how you explore and process your surroundings; write because it's how you aim to understand those people in your life who consternate and amuse you (often the same people) and your own contradictory, complicated self. Connect with the benefits and joys of writing and having written.** There are many ways to get over not-writing guilt—create or join a writing group or work swap, attend a weekend or afternoon workshop, join a class, get a beta reader, or schedule an hour once a week to write beginning this week. Small treats work, too, just saying.

- **Find your tribe and set both personal and group goals. Hang with other writers. We're**

cool! We complain about the same things! We adore a unique turn of phrase! Most importantly: we'll keep each other writing. As Lily Tomlin famously said: "We're all in this together alone." There's plenty of time for the alone at the desk. Cultivate a network, too. [See the above writing group, workshop, class, and beta reader.] Marvellous places I've found other writers on my wavelength include the MFA program I attended at Queens University of Charlotte, NC, readings I've attended and/or participated in, and online classes I've taught. Don't discount making writing friends out of student writers—they are some of the most motivated writing pals I know, and they are still hungrily seeking publication. I teach students from teens through their 80s, so this isn't about age or life situation. Published, unpublished, just starting out, or multiply published—none of this matters, either. It's about reciprocity: meeting others of like minds who will help support our writing journeys as we support theirs. They will help you on days when you think about quitting at least 10 times; they will buy the magazines where your first poems are published; they will keep you laughing when you wonder if you'll ever find an audience or a publisher.

- **Pay attention. Writing ideas are all around; get a Writer's Idea Notebook and/or email ideas to yourself as you encounter them.** So many wondrous ideas occur to us seemingly out of the blue and then just as quickly evaporate. I have one writing friend who could create a sonnet in her head while driving and, without writing it down, recite it for me a week later; 99% of my other writing friends (and myself!) forget an idea one minute after it occurs to me. Unless you're that one rare friend, stack the odds in your favour. Keep paper and pens everywhere, including on your person.

- Publications, nominations, and prizes are all wonderful feathers in the cap, but at base, **write because it's fun and satisfying.** Writing poetry is challenging as well as something which feeds your curiosity and zest for life. **Writing is a life-long apprenticeship with marvel, piece by piece, opening by opening.**

Woot! A Humble, Jumbled, Rollicking Resource List, Just for You:

Websites:

- **The Poetry Foundation,** with craft articles, some audio clips, and a fabulous searchable database of poems: www.poetryfoundation.org/

- The Foundation also publishes the famed ***Poetry magazine***: www.poetryfoundation.org/poetry-magazine

- **The Poetry Society of America,** a huge list of literary journals that specifically seek poems as well as other poetry-writing goodies, including poetry contests: www.poetrysociety.org/psa/poetry/resources/poetry_journals/

- The PSA also has a link of **chapbook publishers**: www.poetrysociety.org/psa/poetry/resources/chapbook_publishers/

- Love Spoken Word? Me, too! Here's the ultimate

resource: **Poetry Out Loud.** Check out resources for teachers, poems & performance, and details about the youth-poetry competition: **www.poetryoutloud.org/**

- **Modern Poetry in Translation** includes links to their magazine, community, translation resources, poems, events, a podcast, and much more: www.mptmagazine.com/

- *Poets & Writers Magazine* **Classifieds,** including contests, editors, workshops, calls for submission, residencies, retreats, and more, and updated/published every other month**: www.pw.org/ classifieds**

- **Poets.org** includes a fantastic database where you can search poems by title and/or author as well as more resources for teachers and information on National Poetry Writing Month. I love their audio and visual clips, along with the Poem-a-Day feature: **www.poets.org/poetsorg/poem-day**

- **Poetry 180,** what began as a project by Poet Laureate Billy Collins in 2001-2003 includes upcoming events, prizes and fellowships, links to the Walt Whitman Collection and Center for the Book, a blog, and more. Also check out two companion anthologies of poems from the project, *Poetry 180: A Turning Back to Poetry* and *180 More: Extraordinary Poems for Every Day,* **both edited by Collins:** www.loc.gov/poetry/180/

- **Tweetspeak Poetry,** daily poems, poetry books, workshops: www.tweetspeakpoetry.com/

- **Unsplendid,** publishes traditional forms, including pantoums, ghazals, Tanka, villanelles, and more: **www.unsplendid.com/subguide_frames.htm**

- **New Pages,** as their tagline states: "NewPages. com is news, information, and guides to literary magazines, independent publishers, creative writing programs, alternative periodicals, indie bookstores, writing contests, and more." Couldn't have said it better myself! www.newpages.com/magazines/big-list-of-lit-mags

Classes/Workshops/Writing Programs:

- **Women on Writing (WOW!),** a vast array of awesome non-credit writing courses for writers of all levels offered online throughout the year, including poetry and other seminars taught by talented, publishing authors and a way to meet fellow poets and potential swap buddies/beta readers: www.wow-womenonwriting.com/WOWclasses.html

- **The Loft,** more cool non-credit writing classes (they also have in-person courses in Minneapolis, Minnesota): www.loft.org/classes/about_online_classes

- **Queens University of Charlotte Low-Residency MFA, amazing and my alma-mater:** www.queens.edu/academics/majors-minors-programs/creative-writing-mfa.html

- Southern New Hampshire University Online MA in English & Creative Writing, professional and inspired: www.snhu.edu/online-degrees/masters/ma-in-english-and-creative-writing

Articles:

- "Thinking Like an Editor: How to Order Your Poetry Manuscript" by April Ossmann www.pw.org/content/thinking_like_an_editor_how_to_order_your_poetry_manuscript_0

- "How to Put Together a Poetry Manuscript for Publication: Transform Your Sheaf of Papers into a Manuscript You Can Submit" by Bob Holman & Margery Snyder www.thoughtco.com/putting-together-a-poetry-manuscript-2725619

Books:
I could catalogue poetry collections, anthologies, and craft books all day, but here's a sampling that has meant much to my students' writing and my own poetic journey:

- *Writing Down the Bones: Freeing the Writer Within* by Natalie Goldberg

- *The Poet's Companion* by Kim Addonizio

- *The Artist's Way* by Julia Cameron

- *Big Magic: Creative Living Beyond Fear* by Elizabeth Gilbert

- *Poemcrazy: Freeing Your Life with Words* by Susan G. Wooldridge

- *New and Selected Poems, Volumes 1 and 2; Blue Iris; the Truro Bear and Other Adventures: Poems and Essays; Red Bird; Thirst* (to name a few) by Mary Oliver

- *Leaves of Grass* by Walt Whitman

- *The Poetry Dictionary* by John Drury

- *Ordering the Storm: How to Put Together a Book of Poems* by Susan Grimm

- *Art & Fear: Observations on the Perils (and Rewards) of Artmaking* by David Bayles & Ted Orland

- *Ode to Common Things, Bilingual Edition*, by Pablo Neruda and Ferris Cook; *Twenty Love Poems and a Song of Despair* and *The Book of Questions* by Pablo Neruda

- *Stag's Leap* and *The Gold Cell* both by Sharon Olds

- *The Poetry Anthology: Ninety Years of America's Most Distinguished Verse Magazine*, edited by Joseph Parisi and Stephen Young

- *How to Read a Poem: And Fall in Love with Poetry* by Edward Hirsch

- *A Book of Luminous Things: An International Anthology of Poetry* by Czeslaw Milosz

- *The Crafty Poet: A Portable Workshop* by Diane Lockward

- *Writing and Enjoying Haiku: A Hands-on Guide* by Jane Reichhold

- *On Being a Writer: 12 Simple Habits for a Writing Life that Lasts* by Ann Kroeker and Charity Singleton Craig

- *Writing the Life Poetic: An Invitation to Read and Write Poetry* by Sage Cohen

- *Narrow Road to the Interior: And Other Writings* by Matsuo Basho, translated by Sam Hamill

Acknowledgements

- Thank you to the following literary journals and venues (and their editors and staff) where some of my included poems were first published: *Germ Magazine* and *Origami Poems Project*. The chapter "Writer in Progress: The Writer's Idea Book, Submission Notebook, and You" appeared previously in a slightly different form in *Fiction Southeast*.

- The following essays appeared in slightly different form under the title: "With Prompts and Patience: The Making of Verse" in *Far Villages: Welcome Essays for New & Beginner Poets* (Black Lawrence Press), edited by Abayomi Animashaun (many thanks, Abayo!):"On Tenacity: 6 Tips for Increased Poetic Productivity," "Crafting Snazzy, Meaningful Titles [of which This Isn't]," "A Green Eel Named Yellow: On (Suspending) Poetic Logic," "The Art of Offering Feedback: Real-World Tips for Helpful Poetry Critiques," and "Will the Real Speaker Please Stand up?"

- For my "Dream Team" at Vine Leaves Press: Jessica Bell and Alexis Paige. Your vision and hard work on behalf of my manuscript has been an honour and a pleasure. Many thanks for your enthusiasm and support while writing and editing this book.

- For graciously sharing his work in this craft book, *merci beaucoup* to Charles A. Swanson, steadfast writing friend and poet. It is a pleasure to read and to showcase your poetry.

- Many thanks to my family—Mom and Dad (Thom and Linda Faith, for endless support and kindnesses innumerable while I pursue my dreams), my favourite first-draft-reader/book-recommender/BBC-devotee/knitter-extraordinare/general-diva-of-awesomeness, Amanda ("Gracie") McGrath, my brother-in-law, Adam, and to my two darling nieces, Cora Vi and Sylvie Ro, who supply me with endless inspiration and humorous remembrances for the journey. I love you very, very much.

- For my readers. Without you, there would be no *Poetry Power!* I look forward to hearing how this book inspired and motivated you, your poetry drafts, and your publishing life. I enjoy hearing from fellow writers. www.melaniedfaith.com/contact/

- Last but certainly not least: for my fellow writers and my writing students. Writing and teaching are my life's work and my legacy, and I appreciate all of your wisdom, insight, and camaraderie during this ongoing writing and teaching life. You have helped me to refine my writing path, and I can think of few adventures more fulfilling and fun than to share what I know and to learn from each of your writing paths. To this continued writing life!

Vine Leaves Press

Enjoyed this book?
Go to *vineleavespress.com* to find more.